how to start a home-based

Quilting Business

how to start a home-based

Quilting Business

Deborah Bouziden

Guilford, Connecticut

Photo on inside front cover by Diane Barker

Editorial Director: Cynthia Hughes Cullen
Editor: Meredith Dias
Project editor: Lauren Szalkiewicz
Text design: Sheryl P. Kober
Layout: Sue Murray

ISBN 978-0-7627-8810-1

Printed in the United States of America

10 9 8 7 6 5 4 3 2 1

This book is dedicated to all those women who design and make quilts. It is especially dedicated to Pearl Harris, who was the inspiration for this book. When I heard her business story, I knew there was a market for other women who wanted to start their quilting business. It is also dedicated to my grandmother, who held a regular quilting bee when I was a child; my mother-in-law, whom I watched sew together a king-size quilt with one-inch squares by hand; and to my mother, who still loves finding new designs and making expertly stitched quilts.

Contents

Acknowledgments

No book of this type or size can be written alone. From its inception to its finish, others helped to make it happen. I'd like to thank the girls at the Golden Quilt Museum and the Golden Quilt Store in Golden, Colorado, for giving me information and pointing me in the right direction to find information. Thanks to Nita Beshear for giving me names of quilters and Patricia Maxwell for not only giving me names but also sending pictures of some of the beautiful quilts she's made. I'd also like to thank the women who spent time answering my questions in interviews: Nita Beshear, Joan Knight, Karen Niemi, Betty Hairfield, Therese May, Rita Meyerhoff, Pearl Harris, Rhonda Ponder, and Melissa Ott-Herman. To those I spoke to at fabric stores and events: Know that your input is just as valued even though I didn't get your names.

My editors, Cynthia Hughes Cullen and Meredith Dias, deserve to be acknowledged as well. Thanks for putting up with my questions, and guiding me through the process. Every writer needs extra eyes. I felt better knowing you two were reading my pages.

Introduction

Think back through the years, and I'm sure you will remember having at least one quilt around you, keeping you warm. Chances are you may remember many. I can, as quilts were staples in our home when I was growing up, and I continued that tradition when I married. I can also remember going to quilting bees as a child, hiding out under the quilts spread across the entire room while my grandmother, her sisters, my mother, and my aunts sewed with needle, thread, and thimble, finishing up quilts to sell.

While new techniques and technology have made the construction of quilts simpler and faster, they have not diminished the pleasure of creating—or of receiving—a handmade quilt. This much-appreciated product has been around for a while. A long while. Most people may be surprised to know that quilting has been around since before Egyptian times. Through the years, quilting has gone through many changes. Early on, it was a specific task performed by workmen. It later evolved into a community- and family-oriented activity.

Today, quilting has become a big business. A 2010 report completed for the Creative Crafts Group indicated that the quilting market was worth an estimated $3.58 billion. According to the report, there were approximately 16.38 million quilting households in the United States alone, and 6.2 percent of those generated 69 percent of quilt-industry spending ($2.48 billion).

With so much income being generated by quilts, it's no wonder many quilters have decided to turn their expertise into income. Today hundreds of home-based quilting businesses operate out of basements, extra bedrooms, and recovered backyard barns across the country. Quilters make money in a diverse range of ways. Besides making and selling their own quilt designs, these entrepreneurs work on a contractual basis to make quilts for others, do quilt restoration, sew sample quilts for quilting and fabric stores to display in their establishments, and finish quilts for those who just want to sew the tops. They teach, design patterns, write books, or even appraise quilts. There are also numerous artists in the quilting field who design and make quilts as art pieces. Manufacturers and suppliers have not turned a blind eye to the home-based quilting business owner; they cater to these businessmen and women.

The list of things quilting business owners can do to supplement their income is quite extensive. However, those who are considering starting a quilting business must be motivated not only to get up and get started every day but to reach out to people, get work done, and maintain accurate records. The ideal owner would not only love quilting, but be willing to interact with people, to enjoy a certain amount of travel, and to do whatever it takes to get jobs completed. Running any type of business is not easy, but if one is willing to work hard, be flexible, and explore multiple options, there is plenty of money to be made in the quilting field.

Home-based Quilting Success Stories

Therese May (theresemay.com) is an art quilter and workshop teacher who does longarm quilting for others. She operates her business out of her home in San Jose, California. She started quilting and designing her own quilts in 1965 after getting some pointers from her husband's grandmother.

"I've always been an artist," May says, "but I got my resale number and business license in 1982 when I started selling more. I make art quilts for walls and also sell small art projects, such as fabric postcards, note cards, ornaments, and patches. The prices range from five dollars to ten thousand dollars."

Collectors seek out May, and she receives commission-based work on a regular basis. She has had numerous one-person exhibits across the United States, and her work has been shown in select group exhibitions in Japan, the Netherlands, and Denmark. In 1999, the quilt she made in 1969 titled "Therese Quilt" was chosen as one of the twentieth century's one hundred best American quilts by a panel of experts from the Alliance for American Quilts, American Quilt Study Group, the International Quilt Association, and the National Quilt Association.

Joan Knight (quiltsandthings.info) of Alabama keeps just as busy as May running her diverse quilting business. A long-time teacher of quilting (since 1993), Knight officially started her business in 2006. She quilts, still teaches, and is an area sales rep for Gammill, a subdealer for the Stitch-n-Frame Gammill dealership, a beta tester for

Creative Studio, and a certified trainer for Creative Studio 4.0. Her studio is located in a "barn" built on her and her husband's property.

"I finish quilts for clients, which range in price from two cents per square inch up to six cents," Knight says. "I also run my teaching business from home, sometimes holding classes for students in the barn. The barn is also home base for my self-produced instructional videos."

Knight has sold baby quilts for one thousand dollars, and she offers national classes for seven hundred dollars per day plus expenses. She does travel; most recently she spent a week in Pennsylvania teaching. She has been honored by the Alabama legislature with a quilt exhibited in the Alabama Artists Gallery with the First Lady of Alabama, Mrs. Robert Bentley. Also, the Japanese magazine, *Patchwork Quilt Tsushin*, published an interview with her about quilting.

Rita Meyerhoff, who owns and operates Heaven's Quilts (heavensquilts.com) in Colorado, has been quilting for about twenty years. She fell in love with the process and was influenced by her grandmother, who loved to sew. She started teaching quilting in 2008. She decided to start her own business, and it has been growing ever since.

"I do a variety of work," Meyerhoff says, "including designing patterns, quilting tops for others, making quilted items for sale (from pincushions for about ten dollars to quilts for five hundred dollars); teaching both private and group classes at quilt shops, quilting guilds, and workshops; speaking publicly regarding quilting, and designing my own quilts."

These ladies as well as others who own and operate their own home businesses are proof that there is money to be made in the making, selling, and teaching of everything "quilt." Many home-based quilting business owners say that they can make anywhere from twenty to one hundred dollars an hour, depending on what they are doing. According to Gammill Industries, "The amount of money a person can make machine quilting will vary due to their location, the type of work clients are willing to pay for, and how many hours a quilter can devote to her business."

Using This Book

We have talked to successful quilting professionals, and we hope that their experience, knowledge, and expertise will help you, a new entrepreneur, build your business. This book will not teach you how to design patterns or how to quilt, but it will offer suggestions on how to run a quilting business. It is designed to give you small pieces of information instead of big chunks. It is divided into sections and then subsections, so you can read through it at a pace that is right for you and then go back and look for specific sections that might require a second look.

This book will help you explore the reasons to start a home-based quilting business, so you can decide if it is right for you, and if so, whether you should run your business as a part-time or full-time venture. We will discuss the pros and cons of your decision and address various issues, such as where you can go to learn special quilting techniques and groups you might want to join to stay up on the latest trends.

Chapters 2 and 3 will include information to help you decide what kind of business you want to own and define the four legal business types available to business owners. In chapter 4 we will explore the different tools and equipment you will need to operate a successful home-based quilting business and what kind of workspace and home office you will need. These chapters will offer suggestions for keeping your tools in tip-top shape and will discuss how you can start your business with what you already have and some bare necessities.

Chapter 5 covers building your support team: bankers, accountants, attorneys, and employees. Chapter 6 provides information on putting together a business plan, why you need one, and what it can do for you. Financial planning and management will be discussed in chapter 7. Here you can also read about how the quilting business differs from other businesses, what to do in lean financial times, and how to prepare for those times by planning ahead when business is exceptionally good.

You will also find a chapter on marketing your business (chapter 8), which discusses everything from word-of-mouth advertising to building a website to getting the word out about your business by networking with guilds and local fabric businesses.

In the back, you will find five appendices. Appendix A is a listing of general resources, including places to find classes or videos to help you improve your skills. Appendix B lists marketing resources, while appendix C lists quilting organizations and guilds as well as agencies that can assist you regarding business matters. Appendix D offers a brief listing of quilting festivals and shows. Finally, appendix E features quilting books that can be found on the Internet, at your local brick-and-mortar bookstore, or at your favorite electronic bookseller.

Running a home-based business is not an easy prospect—many find it to be more challenging than working for an employer—but it does have its rewards. Our goal in this book is to point you in the right direction and bring up issues you may not have thought about before you start your journey. With some forethought, planning, hard work, and motivation, you can have a successful home-based quilting business. We wish you an active, fun-filled, and very profitable future.

01 So You're Thinking about Starting a Home-based Quilting Business

You've thought about this venture for a good long while. Your grandmother made quilts, your aunts and mother made quilts, and you've made quite a number of them yourself. You've got the techniques down, and you love working with fabric. You've considered a quilting business, and, after more careful consideration, you're ready to take the leap.

While it is great that you are excited and filled with enthusiasm at the prospect of your new venture, what do you know about business? If you are going to start your own business, you've got to consider your time, your resources, and your level of commitment. You might want to start by considering these questions:

- Are you married or single?
- How many children do you have and how much time do you need to spend with them? (If they are in high school or grown, you will have more time to spend on your business than if they are young.)
- Will you be able to work evenings and weekends in addition to the days you work during the week?
- How disciplined are you?
- Can you be creative and still have the energy to do the business work that this venture will require?
- Do you have the equipment necessary to run the type of quilting business you want, or do you have capital to invest in new equipment?
- Are you willing to go above and beyond to get your name out there and build your business?

Take some time and think about your answers before you move forward. If you want to start a business, you should go into it with your eyes wide open.

What Kind of Business Are You Starting?

Before you begin, you need to have a clear understanding of exactly what kind of business you are going to start. You may be thinking your business will consist solely of making quilts and selling them, but you need to consider how long it takes to make just *one* quilt. If you can only make three to five quilts a year, that's not going to make you a very big profit. But if you can make one a week and sell each one for approximately five hundred dollars, you may be on to something.

Most of the home-based quilters I've spoken to do a number of things. A quilting business can run the gamut from selling items retail to offering services, such as selling quilts on commission, teaching, or completing quilts for individuals who have started them but are unable to finish. We'll get into more specifics later in the book.

In the meantime, perhaps think about diversifying. This doesn't mean giving up what you love doing, but expanding and growing in your particular field of interest. If you learned quilting techniques from someone and have mastered those techniques, you can probably teach someone else. If you've made quilts from someone else's patterns for a number of years, then you might try designing patterns of your own. What if you love history and quilts equally? Would you consider becoming a quilt historian or appraiser?

You can take your business in many different directions if you are willing to be flexible and think outside a standard pattern for success.

The Whos, Whats, Whens, Wheres, and Whys of a Quilting Business

So, let's get down to the basics.

Who can run a quilting business? Anyone, man or woman. However, with that comes a caveat. The person who is thinking about starting a quilting business better have had some experience sewing and have made more than one or two quilts already. People will come to you with questions, and you want to be able to answer those questions when they come up.

When it comes to looking at *what* can be quilted or sold in the quilting field, the list is enormous. You can sell quilted items—baby quilts, baby bibs, purses, bags, pillows, table runners, designer quilts, kit quilts, apparel, and more. You can also market books, patterns, and quilt kits. Services rendered can range from teaching quilt making to finishing quilts for those who just make the tops.

The great thing about this business is you can do it anytime, so the *when* is easy to answer. One thing to keep in mind about the when, though, is that your business will tend to vary seasonally. In the summer, not many people will be thinking about snuggling up under a quilt, but the summer may be the perfect time for you to take part in a fair, festival, or quilt show. In the winter, around the beginning of December, you will want to have plenty of items already made for purchase as Christmas gifts. By varying your activities according to the ebb and flow of people's buying habits you will be ready to sell when your customers are ready to buy.

Your quilting business can be operated from any*where*, east coast to west, in the city or country, in a basement or a barn. While it is true that you can run your business any*where*, even from your kitchen table, if you are seriously thinking about making this a business, you need to have a dedicated spot of your own—one that gives you enough space to cut, design, sew, send out orders, and, yes, take on new ones.

As for the *whys* of being a home-based quilting business owner, I hope that your first reason is that you love quilting and feel that running a business and sharing your love of quilting with others is the perfect fit for you. You can be successful at any business you love as long as you are aware it will take a while to build up your reputation and, therefore, your business. You have to really want to do this and be committed to doing it for the long haul.

If you want to start your own business because you think it will be easier than having a nine-to-five job—no boss telling you what to do, doing things your way, and no office politics—think again. There are just as many negatives in owning and running your own business as there are in working for someone else.

Running your own business means that you are where the buck stops. If there is no money coming in, then you either haven't been promoting your business or you haven't been making quilts to sell. If you are sick, then there is no one to take up the slack. If you currently work for a company, you probably get insurance, worker's compensation, and your taxes taken out when you get paid. When you work for yourself, you are responsible for everything. You are the bottom line.

If you've given a great deal of thought to this adventure, you might be ready to start your own business. You will be your own boss, set your own hours, and be the soul determiner of how much money you can and will make. Now, let's take a closer look at your motives.

Do You Have What It Takes to Be a Quilting Business Owner?

Before you jump in, let's look at a few questions to see if you are ready. Think about each question and answer honestly. These are questions for you and you alone because you know yourself better than anyone else. No one is going to be standing next to you, prodding you about how you should answer. You know your strengths, and knowing them can take you far, but you need to know your limitations too.

Owning your own business can be fun. It can also be stressful. Problems can and will arise. How you handle those problems can make or break your business. How will you handle stress? How will you deal with unexpected problems? Take the time to answer the thirteen questions below and see if you are cut out to own and operate a quilting business:

1. **What kind of training have you had to work in the quilting business?** You don't need a college degree to own and operate a quilting business. However, you do need a basic knowledge of sewing, color management, quilting techniques, and the experience of having made a number of quilts yourself. Because you will be operating a business, people will look to you as an expert and come to you with questions. It would be wise for you to know how to answer them.

2. **What kind of business experience do you have?** Do you know how to fill out tax reports? Have any bookkeeping experience? Have you ever worked in a retail setting? If you don't have any business experience, do you know someone who can help you, or do you have time to attend some of the Small Business Association's workshops? This isn't a big hurdle to jump, but you do need to get some guidance if you have no idea what you are doing. There will be assets and inventory to keep track of and expenditures that will need to be tracked for the Internal Revenue Service and state tax offices.

3. **How is your health?** While you don't need to be an Olympic athlete, you do need to be in fairly good health. If you've been diagnosed with a major disease or an illness that zaps your energy all the time, starting a business right now might not work. Dealing with an illness is rough, and starting a new business can add stresses to your life just when you need to eliminate sources of worry and tension. All the effort could wear you down.

4. **Are you a self-starter?** When you own your own business, you will not have anyone telling you what to do or when to do it. You will need to be at your computer or sewing machine at eight in the morning and stay until the job is done. You will be the person who is ordering or going out to find the fabric you will need for the next project. You will be the one making the phone calls and following up with people who have placed orders and hired you for projects.

> **Patchwork**
>
> Set up a daily schedule to do certain tasks, such as answering business e-mail first thing in the morning. This will get you into a routine so that you won't miss commission work or orders you can fill that day.

5. **Can you be flexible, yet stay focused?** Because of the nature of your business, you may be forced to do many different things during a typical day. You may be designing or making a quilt when the phone rings and you have to take an order that needs to be shipped immediately. Will you be able to stop what you are doing and come back to your original task later without missing a beat?

6. **How are your organizational skills?** To be successful in any business, you must maintain a certain level of organization. You will need to know where your patterns are and which fabrics will need to be washed, ironed, cut, and ready to sew. You will need to keep addresses of both customers and suppliers organized and handy. You'll also need to neatly maintain your files so that whenever you need something, you don't spend half the morning looking for it.

7. **Do you like to sew and work with fabric?** Because you will be working with other quilters or making quilts yourself, your sewing machine had better be your best friend. You should think of fabric the way writers think about words and artists think about paints or canvases. If you hate working with fabric, and the thought of sitting at the sewing machine day after day makes you feel nauseated, you probably should think of something else to do.

8. **How are you at figuring out puzzles?** Putting together a quilt is like doing a jigsaw puzzle. In many respects, running a business is like that too. You start out with a vision of what you want to do and where you want to go, and then you try to use the pieces you have to make it all come together. Thinking about the challenges your business may throw at you and being prepared for them will help you see your vision more clearly and reach your business goals.

9. **Can you motivate yourself?** Let's be honest: There are going to be days when you don't feel like working. Perhaps an order didn't come in, you have no

orders to work on, or you just got through a busy weekend and Monday came too soon. Instead of sitting around doing nothing all day, you will need to track down orders, perhaps go the fabric store and buy replacement fabric, do some online marketing or leave your cards at stores, and write out your weekly goals and to-do list. Can you do it? Can you work even though you might not feel like it?

10. **Do you feel you can commit to this long term?** If you are thinking about starting this business for a year to see how it does, go find a job working somewhere else. A business is a commitment—a long-term commitment. It may take a year or more before your name starts getting out to the public, and it may take three to five years before you start to make a noticeable profit. You wouldn't go into a marriage thinking that you might want to try something else after a year. You shouldn't start a business with that attitude, either.

11. **Are you persistent?** Salesmen say that it takes ten people who say no before one decides to buy their product. You may pass out fifty business cards and not get one bite, or you may go to ten fairs or festivals before anyone buys your products. At times like these, are you willing to hang tough, keep passing out your cards, or showing up at events until you do make a sale?

12. **What kind of constitution do you have?** Do you work well under pressure? Do you have a good attitude about life overall? Having a positive and happy outlook will help you go far. First, no one wants to work with a sourpuss. Second, if you are prone to depression or angry outbursts when things don't go your way, you might want to rethink the whole home-based business idea. Obstacles and roadblocks will happen. Just when you think everything is moving along at a good pace, your electricity will go off because of a freak accident or sudden snowstorm and your sewing machine won't work. If you can stay calm amid turmoil, you will be happy and get more work done in the long run.

13. **Can you allow yourself to make mistakes and improve after making them?** Even large corporations have problems, and so will you. When you run your own business, mistakes are going to happen, not only with the work itself, but on the business end as well. Be prepared for it. You might finish a quilt and discover the colors are all wrong. Maybe you promised a client a product by a certain date, but you come down with the flu and are in bed

for three weeks. Perhaps you mail off a quilt and find you've sent it to the wrong address. If you had visions of having your own business because you thought everything would run smoothly all the time, think again. Things will happen. If you can't live with mistakes and dealing with them when they happen, then a home-based quilting business may not be the best business for you.

How did you do with these questions? While you may not have answered yes to every one, you should have done so for most of them. If you did, you are probably a good fit for the quilting business. If not, don't be discouraged. No one knows everything. You may just need to start small or do some research or spend some time learning about business and quilting in general, and then revisit your goals in a year or so. Owning and running a business is a big commitment. You can manage it if you face your shortcomings head on and commit to working on them.

Beyond Design

Nita Beshear owner of *A Patchwork Life,* a quilting business in Oklahoma, says, "The biggest advantage of owning and operating a home-based business is I can make my own schedule. If I need to go babysit my grandkids, go visit them, or go to a quilt show, I don't have to get approval from a boss. The work will still be here when I return, or I will need to work harder before leaving, but the time is mine. The biggest disadvantage is that I am responsible for everything: taxes, healthcare, upkeep on my machines, and more."

A Day in the Life of a Quilting Business Owner

You've decided this is what you want to do, so let's take a look at what a typical day for you might be like. We will look at two scenarios: 1) where you have an online store, and 2) where you finish quilts for clients using a longarm machine and make samples for fabric stores.

Scenario 1

In the first scenario, you start your day around eight o'clock in the morning, meaning you are in the office or your work area by then. You head to your computer, coffee cup in hand, and look at the orders received overnight or review the ones you got the day before. After entering all the information into a spreadsheet, you print it off, double-check to see if the customers' credit cards went through, gather envelopes, and see if you have the materials you need to fill your current orders.

This takes about an hour. You decide you can fill 50 percent of your orders, but you'll have to cut some more fat quarters and print off patterns for the other 50 percent.

It's about half past nine when you go back to your computer to print out invoices and address labels for the orders you can fill today. After getting all your paperwork, you head over to your worktable, where you will ready the envelopes and fill the orders you can. You stack the ones you've completed in the post office container and check those off your list. In between all your other things to do, you are answering the phone and any inquiries that may come via e-mail.

By now, depending on the size of your orders, it's around ten thirty or eleven. You decide to pull out the materials you need to fill some of your other orders and set to work gathering fabric, scissors, ribbon, and any other needed items. After cutting enough fabric for a few more orders, you realize you are out of a specific fabric. You leave things where they are and jot a quick list, gather your packages to be mailed, and head out to the fabric store and post office. Here is where you might want to think about taking a lunch. You can grab something at home or pick up something while you are out and about.

Two and a half hours later, you are back home, fabric in hand, and ready to do some more cutting. You'll only get about an hour's work completed because it's already four o'clock. After supper is over, you'll be back in your work area, cutting and putting together more orders. You need to get the current ones done before the new orders come in.

You finally leave your work area at about nine o'clock, too tired to do anything else for the night. Tomorrow morning, you will start all over again.

Time	Task
8:00 a.m.	Arrive at your home office.
8:00 to 9:30 a.m.	Review all orders and enter information into spreadsheets.
9:30 to 11:00 a.m.	Print out invoices/address labels and fill orders. Answer phone calls and e-mails.
11:00 a.m. to 1:00 p.m.	Prepare fabric.
1:00 to 1:30 p.m.	Eat lunch.
1:30 to 4:00 p.m.	Run errands (fabric store, post office, etc.).
4:00 to 5:00 p.m.	Cut fabric.
5:00 to 6:00 p.m.	Eat supper.
6:00 to 9:00 p.m.	Return to your workspace to do more cutting and fill more orders.
9:00 p.m.	Stop working for the day.

Scenario 2

Now, if you have the second kind of business, you will still start your day early in the morning at eight o'clock as well. Because you are finishing quilts for people who have already made the top, you will set up the quilt with its batting and back, roll it into your machine, check your thread (making sure the tension is right), check your pattern, and get started. Your goal is to get this one finished today. Fortunately, your customers have sent backing material for the three quilts due next.

You spend the morning working the longarm machine. At about ten o'clock, it runs out of thread, so you spend time rethreading it and getting going again. After finishing up one, you unpack other quilt tops and read notes and e-mails from other clients. In between occasional phone calls, you also put the finishing touches on the presentation you are going to give to the new fabric store for which you hope to sew sample quilts. You have to meet the owner at one o'clock this afternoon.

While you eat a quick lunch, you update a few pages on your website, work on an ad you're considering running next week in a national women's magazine, and gather the materials you need for your meeting.

You arrive at the meeting a few minutes early and prepare yourself. The meeting lasts about an hour, and it looks promising. The manager gives you the pattern for a baby blanket she wants you to make for a display. Before you leave the fabric store, you look for the material you'll need, purchase it, and look for backing for a quilt that doesn't have any yet. Your client is familiar with your work, so she has left the decision of what color and pattern up to you.

You head back home about three o'clock. You finish putting another quilt on the longarm machine and then get back on your computer to answer e-mail and firm up details about the samples you will be making for the retail store.

Although you still want to work on some quilting designs, you take a break to eat something for supper and then you're back in your workspace, at your computer by half past six. You work a few more hours and finish up at about nine o'clock. You're done for the day, but you'll be back at it tomorrow at eight in the morning.

As you think about this venture, keep in mind that you will basically be doing the same thing every day. Sure, the routine will vary on occasion, but you should be taking care of your customers and clients first thing each day. They are the ones making you money, and if you ignore them, your profits will slip.

Your Workday: Sample Schedule 2

Time	Task
8:00 a.m.	Arrive at your home office.
8:00 to 10:00 a.m.	Prepare quilting materials and work on your longarm machine.
10:00 a.m. to 12:30 p.m.	Rethread the longarm machine to finish your first quilt. Respond to phone calls and e-mails. Unpack materials for next projects.
12:30 to 12:45 p.m.	Eat lunch, update your website, and gather materials for your meeting.
1:00 p.m.	Attend a meeting with the owner of a new fabric store.
3:00 to 5:30 p.m.	Put another quilt into the longarm machine and answer more e-mails.
5:30 to 6:30 p.m.	Eat dinner.
6:30 to 9:00 p.m.	Finish up miscellaneous tasks.
9:00 p.m.	Stop working for the day.

What Kind of Work Can the Quilting Business Owner Find?

In this line of work, as mentioned earlier, you will want to diversify to a certain degree. How quickly you make product and what kind of product that is will determine not only what kind of money you will be making but the possible range of your work. Other factors that will affect the range of your business include whether you will be working alone or have individuals who help you on either a part- or full-time basis. Of course, first you'll have to have work for employees to do and enough profit to support them. In planning income streams for your business, you will only be limited by your own goals and thoughts. There are many places to find commissions, clients, and customers if you are willing to do the work and look for them. You don't have to decide right away which areas you want to cover. Start small with one or two services—perhaps making log-cabin quilts and cutting fat-quarter kits to sell on the Internet. Once you get going, you may want to expand your offerings. Perhaps teaching would fit the bill. Even if teaching in a class setting makes you uncomfortable, you could always try taking on clients one at a time in private classes.

In the next few pages, we summarize types of quilters, so you can consider opportunities you might want to investigate. This is in no way an all-inclusive list. As technology advances and creative individuals come up with new ideas for the art of quilt making, other opportunities will present themselves. Always be looking for something that gets you excited. Be realistic, but if you think you might be good in a particular area and want to try it, calculate the cost and jump in.

Longarm Quilter

Quite a few quilters have formed side businesses to finish up quilts for people who have only made the top part of a quilt. These clients may only be interested in making the tops, lack the money or time to own a quilting machine, or have too many quilt tops they need finished. These types of business owners own longarm machines. (We'll talk about the machines in chapter 2.)

A quilter who owns a longarm machine can realistically finish one to two quilts a day, depending on the complexity and size of the quilt. Charges can range from fifty to one hundred dollars just for the service of quilting the project. Most customers will include the batting and back material. Without the batting and back, the price you quote will be higher. Then there is the charge for postage.

One quilter who runs a longarm business also offers to finish the edges of the quilts for her clients. Some clients want her to do this, while others choose to do it themselves. When clients aren't sure, she offers them an estimate and lets them decide.

A longarm quilting business can keep you busy. At one point, this particular quilter was a week behind because of the number of quilt tops she'd had come in. She has built up her business over the years and has a good reputation for quality work.

Commission Quilter

If you want commissions to be part of your business, you will need to get special orders from individuals and make quilts for them. These could be of your own design, or your clients could see a pattern and want you to make a quilt from it. You would typically have your name out there, as well as a website with photos of quilts you've done in the past. No doubt a business like this does well with word-of-mouth advertising; if you have made quilts for others who like them and think you gave them a good price, they will spread the word. Just know ahead of time that you may go for months without orders and then suddenly have ten.

Depending on what you like to quilt, you could specialize in a specific area. There are log cabin, crazy, or appliqué quilts, to name a few. If you have made and are familiar with all the categories, you will probably be diversified enough to make anything a client may want. But if you've only made log cabin quilts, then you might want to specialize in and base your business on making them.

Your clients will probably want you to estimate how much the quilt will cost. Remember to include not only your time and labor, but also the cost of materials. Commissioned quilts may range in price from two hundred to one thousand dollars, depending on what materials you have to purchase, how complex the design is, and how long it will take you.

Know in advance that when clients get estimates, they may reconsider when they hear the price. After getting a go-ahead from a client, make sure you collect 50 percent up front or get the entire cost of the materials. You don't want to invest all your money in a project only to have the client not want it when it is finished. At least if you've collected for the materials, you can sell the blanket to compensate for your invested time if you have to.

Casual Quilter

Maybe you are just starting out and want to quilt without any pressure. You don't care if you have orders or not. You just want to make the quilts you want to make and sell them when they are made. There's nothing wrong with that if you are motivated and can keep your enthusiasm and focus up when distractions come along. Most people find it difficult to stay on track if they don't have a deadline, and a client's order gives them a deadline.

However, casual quilting might be a good place to start. You can find out how long it takes you to make the type of quilt you are interested in. You will also know in advance of your setting the price what the materials cost you. After you make the quilt, you can put it up on your website and start marketing it. Of course, the more finished quilts you have up on your website, the more traffic you will get. By having ten to fifteen to start, you will give your customers more to choose from and give yourself time to make more quilts. Going about your business this way will also give you time to decide if you want to participate in fairs and festivals around your area. Quilters do pretty well when they sell their wares at craft fairs and shows.

Art Quilters (Fiber Artists)

Another category would be the artist quilter or fiber artist. These quilters design and make their own quilts, put pictures up on their websites, and sell the quilts online and at art shows. These quilts are intricate, and many designs have won prizes and awards. Art quilters can—and do—charge exorbitant prices for their quilts. The prices range from one or two thousand to tens of thousands of dollars.

Because these quilters typically make one of a kind quilts, it is difficult to reproduce another exactly the way an original was made. The price of an art quilter's products depends on their originality and uniqueness. However, if a client likes the quilt artist's style, he may want to commission the artist to make a quilt using similar colors, or fabric (e.g., silk, etc.).

If you have some knowledge of the art world and already have an established reputation, this will help your cause if you decide to venture into this area. You will want to enter your quilts in art shows and contests. The more the public is exposed to your art and the more shows or contests you win, the higher the prices you can get for your work.

Producer of Quilted Items

If you like to quilt but feel that quilts are too big for you to tackle right now or would take too much of your time, you could start your business by selling small quilted items such as baby blankets, bibs, purses, wallets, table runners, and more. These would take fewer materials and less time, yet still get you started in the business. You could do quite well with these items, as people are always looking for gift items. If you set the right prices and marketing strategy, you may find that small items are where you want to specialize.

You could start with several small items and then specialize in those items that are most popular. A number of quilters have done this with purses and are doing quite well selling just them. One person uses upholstery material to make her bags and purses. She sells out regularly, and her products range in price from $35 all the way to $350. She travels to shows and festivals and also has a website where individuals can purchase her products.

You should be able to sell your items for prices ranging from ten to two hundred dollars. Because you will invest less time in these smaller items, you will still have time to make full-size quilts throughout the year.

Quilt Pattern Designer

People are always looking for new and fresh patterns. If you like to experiment with color and design, solve puzzles, or create something from nothing, perhaps you might explore starting a business where you sell your own designs and patterns. With quilt designing software, making your own patterns and designs couldn't be easier and more challenging at the same time—easier because of the software, but also more challenging to come up with something unique and to design it so that it will work with the program and match what you have in mind.

Once you have your designs made, you can make your own patterns or have them printed for you. From there it is a small step to put them up on the Internet or perhaps peddle your original designs to local fabric stores. You could even go one step further and sell your designs and patterns as kits.

You could grow in a variety of ways. You could start out with simple kits for the beginning quilter and then branch out to more complex quilt patterns for the more experienced quilter. You could also design quilt patterns that follow a specific theme. If you like rabbits, why not do a series of rabbit quilt patterns? After you have ten or twelve patterns and have made those quilts, query a publishing house about getting your patterns published in book form. This will only enhance your status as a quilt pattern designer.

Quilting Teacher

Once you have honed your skills and become proficient at what you do, you might want to consider teaching some quilting classes. You can start by teaching those who want to learn how to sew or who are interested in making their first quilt. These classes don't have to be extravagant and can help you see if you like to teach.

Not everyone is cut out to be an instructor. A lot of the work takes place before the class, when you are preparing for the class. You might have to cut out materials for your students or write up class instructions.

You will also have to choose how long you want the class to run. Will it be a Saturday morning class or an all-day Saturday class? If it is to be held during the week in the evenings, how long will the classes run—four weeks, six weeks, or eight? You could start with one class but have several more lined up. If students like your first class, they will sign on for more.

Remember when setting up your class that an all-day Saturday class can be quite exhausting. You will need to allow time for breaks. By the end of the day, everyone will be tired, so plan the challenging moments in the morning when everyone is fresh.

Students will come to your classes at different learning levels and with different skills. Some will be able to follow instructions and move along easily. Others will need extra attention and will slow down your other students. Think about this in advance and decide how you will handle those situations.

Think too about how long it will reasonably take one of your students to finish a project. A project that may take you a few hours may take your students twice as long. The number of students in your class will also be important in deciding how long a class will be. Depending on everyone's skill level, a class of six to ten is generally good. If you get more than ten, some students may end up feeling neglected.

There is an upside to limiting your classes. If your classes start filling up, you may have to start a waiting list or hold two classes. You could do one Saturday morning and one Saturday afternoon. You could also do classes on Monday and Thursday evenings.

No matter what classes you decide to teach, keep in mind that your students will want to be challenged. Whether they are taking a one-day class or a series of eight classes, they will feel better about themselves and the classes if they can take home a completed project at the end. Many projects that aren't finished by the end of class won't ever get finished.

When pricing your classes, you will need to factor in the supplies provided, your facility fee, and your hourly fee. Check around to see what other instructors are charging. If you are just starting out, you might want to drop your price five dollars below the going rate. This will help you get students. After you get a few classes under your belt, you can raise your fees.

Quilting Author

Another lucrative source of income, and an avenue to boost your teaching business, is writing books and getting them published. Many quilters choose to write quilt pattern books focusing on a specific kind of quilt, but there are also books on the history of quilts and quilting techniques—or a combination of the three areas.

Don't count yourself out by thinking your book idea has already been written. You just have to write a better, clearer one and put your own personal spin on it. Another quilting book hits the market every week. Yours just has to be different.

You may want to start small and begin by writing articles for magazines or your local newspaper. One good way to write a book is to write many different articles and then combine them into a book after you have written a number of them.

It takes a long time to write a book, so don't think this is something that will happen overnight. It is one of those things you will have to incorporate into everything else you do. Once you do get a book published, however, people will begin to see you as an expert in your field. You'll get more students in your classes and no doubt will begin picking up speaking engagements. That is a good thing because at these events and classes, you will be able to sell your books and other products, thus generating more revenue for yourself.

Online Store Owner

Online stores can make good profits for home-based businesses. After getting a website made and preparing your projects or products, you can go live and start selling items. You will need to decide what kinds and types of products you are going to sell. Will your site be a place where people can come and buy only patterns? Will you have quilting supplies available, such as scissors and sewing machines? Will you be selling already quilted products (such as quilts, purses, and table runners), quilting kits, or a combination of items?

Don't think this is an easy business. While there are programs out there that will automatically take orders for you, in the end someone has to fill the orders and ship them. Then there is the matter of advertising, updating your website, staying in contact with your customers, and keeping up with the inventory you send out.

Quilt Retreat and Cruise Organizer

If you like working with people, quilts, and planning big parties, perhaps this area might be a good fit for you. In this job, you would be responsible for organizing and arranging a place, time, cost, length, and everything in between for people to get together and improve their sewing and quilting skills. You will need to know something about tourism and the places where you will be arranging the retreats, conferences, or cruises. Thinking that a place would make a nice retreat area doesn't necessarily make it so. Will it be big enough to accommodate the group you will be bringing? Will there be enough space for classes and sewing?

You will also need to have some negotiating skills. When you find a venue, you will need to negotiate not only your meeting space, but the rooms your participants will be staying in. All your hard work won't do you any good if no one can afford to attend.

Once you've locked down a location, you will need to create an itinerary, invite guest speakers, and choose a theme for your event. All this should be done at least a year in advance. The following months will need to be spent on advertising. If your first event is a success, you will have returning guests and your numbers will grow.

Quilt Show Manager

How are your organizational skills? If you have a knack for getting things to run smoothly amid chaos, you might want to try your hand at being a quilt show organizer. There are hundreds of shows across the United States alone every year, and there are always organizations looking for individuals to manage them.

You might have to start small and organize your local group's quilt show for the price of admission, but with each one you work, you will learn valuable tips on how to improve things. Starting small will also help you decide if you like this type of work or would prefer to do something that involves less hassle.

Quilt Appraiser, Historian, or Consultant

If you have any background in history and the fiber arts, you might want to consider a quilt appraising or consultant business. If a client is interested in antiques and the historical significance of older quilts, he or she might call on you not only to authenticate a quilt's age, but also to appraise its worth.

You could work with museums, antique dealers, or private collectors. As a consultant, you would be telling your clients the best way to care for and store their collections and where they could send items for restoration.

While there isn't a large need for this type of work, not many people have a background in history and fiber arts. You could plan to specialize in one area, such as Civil War collections or baby quilts through the ages.

Quilt Restorer

Another area you might want to consider is quilt restoration. Just like someone who restores an antique piece of furniture, you would be responsible for keeping the integrity of the piece while repairing anything torn, discolored by fire or water damage, or damaged by time and location. If you are impatient and like things done quickly so that you can move on to other projects, this is probably not the line of work for you.

You will be something of a detective because, when you receive a job, you will need to do some background research, find out how old the quilt may be, what materials were originally used, and where you can get the same fabrics and materials. Know too that you will be repairing these quilts in the fashion they were made, so there will probably not be any machine quilting involved. It will all have to be completed by hand.

Quilt Show Judge

Once you have established yourself as an expert in this field, you might want to offer your services as a quilt show judge. This will give you exposure not only to people in your field, but the public in general.

To do this job, you need to have made a number of quilts yourself, entered quilt shows, won prizes, and know, *really* know, about pattern and sewing techniques. There are criteria not just for the contestants, but for the judges as well.

Because quilt shows are held all over the world, you should be able to find one to judge in your local area. Be ready to be scrutinized for your skills and have a recommendation letter or two ready for the organizers. It is better if someone has recommended you to the organizing committee, but don't be shy about sending in a letter so you can be considered.

This will be another one of those areas you will want to incorporate into your skill set, as quilt show judges are typically not needed year-round. This will get your name out among the public, however, and help you sell your books, classes, or products.

Moving from Amateur to Professional

Making quilts for friends and loved ones is definitely a way to get experience in sewing and quilt making, but now you've decided to join a competitive business world and start earning money—instead of oohs and ahhs and pats on the back—doing what you love. (Of course, you hope the accolades will continue.) You may not be able to charge the big bucks at first, but the point is to begin somewhere.

Another decision you need to make as a business owner is whether you want to work at this part-time or full-time. It's probably best to start off part-time. Right now, you might need your present job for the extra income to buy machinery or supplies. Once you get enough orders and have enough contacts to replace your present salary, then you can move over to a full-time position. Starting and building a business takes time. Don't expect to be making what you make at your current job in the first month. The key to this, as well as to any other successful business, is persistence.

Perhaps, you don't have a current full-time job. You've been a homemaker, taking care of your children, making quilts on the side. Now your last child has entered school. You have all the equipment and supplies you need to get started full time, so by all means jump in with both feet.

Once you do begin, where do you go to learn more skills or how to run a business? A lot of quilters out there have learned by taking a class here and a class there. Maybe they have been fortunate enough to have mothers, grandmothers, or aunts who have quilted and learned as they were growing up. There aren't any quilting schools, but there are still ways to expand your knowledge, not only with your quilting skills, but your business skills as well.

On-the-Job Training

Because there isn't a brick-and-mortar quilting school, you will learn most things on the job as you go. You have probably been making quilts or quilted projects for a number of years, and that is the reason you decided to start your own business. Perhaps you saw a niche that needed to be filled and knew you could fill it. The more quilts you make, the more patterns you design, and the more questions you answer, the more experience you will gain. You will learn what threads work with which materials and which is the fastest and most economical way to lay out and cut patterns.

If you are hesitant to be completely on your own, look for a mentor to study with for a few years. Don't expect to learn everything your mentor knows, but watch and learn everything you can and then practice, practice, practice. Every new skill and technique you master will benefit you and your business in the future.

Another way to get some on-the-job training is to volunteer. There are organizations that sew quilts for children (Quilts for Kids, quiltsforkids.org) and several for veterans and combat personnel (Quilts of Valor, qovf.org; Quilts of Honor, quiltsofhonor.org; and Quilts for Vets, kellytrudell.net/vetsupport/quiltsforvets.html). Volunteering for such organizations will teach you how to work on a schedule and work within parameters clients may set in your own business. This is also a good way to mix and mingle with people who share your interests.

Don't think volunteering is a waste of your time. You never know whom you'll meet and what contacts you will make—and, in your line of work, you need contacts. We'll talk more about contacts and networking in chapter 8.

Seminars, Conferences, and Workshops

Throughout the year, there are many quilting seminars, workshops, and various conferences in different parts of the country. You can attend these events to continue expanding your skills. The National Quilting Association (nqaquilts.org) holds an annual quilt show where you can mix and mingle, learn about new products and techniques, and take classes on how to implement that information in your business.

Check with your local fabric or quilt store to find out who might offer classes or workshops in your area. Even if you have to drive thirty minutes to go to a class, it may be worth the information you pick up and the experience you gain. Also check with places like Jo-Ann Fabric and Craft and Hobby Lobby. These stores offer sewing classes and many times will expand them into quilting classes. If there are no classes listed, ask the owner or manager for recommendations. There might be someone in your area who will give one-on-one quilt classes.

Self-Study

In today's electronic and digital age, there is no excuse for anyone not to be knowledgeable in the field they want to pursue. For the quilter, there are books on everything from making your first quilt to color study to technique, DVD series, online classes, and the ever present YouTube. Just Google "online quilt classes" and you will find a plethora of suggestions. Look through them to see which one would be right for you and sign up if you can afford it.

The key to self-study is to learn all you can about what you are interested in and to always keep learning. Read and listen to everything you can. Go to the library and check out books on color, sewing techniques, quilt history, and quilt making. You would be amazed what you can learn about quilt making from the history of quilts.

Also check out quilting magazines. Subscribe to a couple that you feel are at your expertise level. Not only will these magazines have patterns and techniques, but they will keep you up to date on new products coming out, quilt shows, and new programs.

The more events and classes you attend and the more quilt-oriented groups you join, the more contacts you will make. Many times, groups or organizations will have lending libraries that lend books or DVDs. Don't be afraid to ask. You may never know unless you do.

Another place to check for educational material is museums. The Rocky Mountain Quilt Museum in Golden, Colorado, has a library filled with resources. While museums may not be solely devoted to quilts, if they have annual quilt exhibits, chances are they'll have information in their archives about the topic.

Finding and Attending Degree Programs and Classes

People interested in quilting as a profession will be hard-pressed to find a school or college that offers a formal quilting degree. But don't despair. You can get a bachelor of fine arts in textiles or a bachelor of arts in design or fiber arts through a four-year undergraduate program at various colleges like Michigan State University, Baylor University, and the Fashion Institute of Technology. You might also want to consider a master of arts in textile history with a focus on quilting.

While these programs are not easy to find, they do exist. For those interested in following up on this, you might want to look up The Studio Art Quilt Associates (saqa.com). The website includes a list of fiber art degree programs.

If a degree isn't your goal but knowledge is, check with local technical schools. There are a few across the country that offer courses in quilting. They don't offer degrees or certification, but you can learn how to quilt and the stitching required for quilting. You can also learn about different pattern types, how to choose fabrics, how to calculate seams and fabric requirements, and more. You will need to read the description of the class carefully before you decide to participate. If your goal is to become educated in the process of quilt making, technical school classes may be a better financial choice for you anyway.

Prices for classes, no matter what they are, will vary from class to class and by location. Don't be afraid to ask questions about the class if you're not sure what is being offered. You don't want to get in a class that's way beneath you, but you don't want one in which you are struggling, either. If you're not sure, contact the instructor and ask about the level of instruction.

For those who may not be able to find an accessible school or training program, you might want to consider joining the American Quilt Study Group (AQSG, american-quiltstudygroup.org). This group is devoted to the study and research of quilt artistry and its history. The group offers scholarships to people who do quilting research and has a large online community that discusses groups and educational resources.

Another way to find the education you want—maybe the best way—is to ask around and find those who have been down the path you want to follow. These people can offer suggestions, and then it's up to you to follow through by researching those areas. Whether you want to be a quilt artist, historian, or make the best quilts in the nation, your education and your success are up to you.

You don't need to have a college degree to be successful in this field, but you have to think of yourself as a success no matter what level of education you have. If you tend to be insecure or shy away from one area, then perhaps that is the area you need to work on. If you feel confident in what you do and the level of knowledge you have, then you can dive in and get started.

A word of caution here: Don't ever think you know everything and quit learning. It is wise to attend conferences and workshops regularly to find out what's new. It's the only way to stay ahead of your competition. It may not change the design of your business, but if you can find a better way to advertise, a quicker way to cut out patterns, or how to use your machine more efficiently, I think it is worth your time.

Business Education

If you've never worked in a business or had any business training, that may be the place to start in this new venture. Many businesses fail, not because the owners do not have a good idea or product, but because they do not use good business practices. It's just as important for you to have business savvy as it is for you to know about your quilts. Government rules and regulations change from year to year—and in some cases from month to month. It's important to keep track of all the changes that might affect your business, from social security withholding to insurance regulations.

There are many places you can go to learn about running a business. Junior colleges, vocational-technical schools, business and trade schools, and even libraries offer business education through their continuing education departments. These classes are usually held in the evenings and on weekends, making it more convenient for those who work to attend. Classes will vary from computer education, small business management, and bookkeeping to marketing and advertising your business. In some areas, communities offer weekend workshops for small business owners. You should also be able to find books on running a small business at your local bookstore and library.

The Small Business Administration (SBA), the federal agency that helps small businesses, will probably be your greatest source for small business information. The agency's website (sba.gov) has all sorts of material you can download: forms, small business journals, information on business loans, and much more. The SBA also offers online support in business management, finance and accounting, and what you can do to survive today's sluggish economy.

If you would like to speak with someone face to face, the SBA has Small Business Development Centers (SBDCs) located across the United States. These centers assist new business owners with immediate counseling on matters relating to their businesses, such as running the business, getting started, marketing, and financial matters.

The Women's Business Center is another resource available through the SBA. This agency helps women through counseling and training on how to help them build their businesses and make them successful.

According to the SBA, their largest resource partner is the Service Corps of Retired Executives (SCORE). SCORE is represented by thirteen thousand volunteers who have business experience in over six hundred business fields. Some are retired, and others are working executives, small business owners, or corporate business owners who volunteer and share their expertise with new business owners.

Each year, SCORE volunteers help thousands of new businesses get started. They hold local workshops and offer face-to-face counseling as well as online training. Since 1964, SCORE has helped over nine million people start their businesses. Go to score.org to find an office near you.

As you begin to look, you will find that there is a lot of information out there on running and maintaining your business. The caveat to that is you have to be willing to look, ask for help when you get stumped, and pursue any direction that may help you find what you're looking for. Some people think that asking for help will make them look weak, when actually the opposite is true. By asking for help you will find the answers you seek and build your business on a solid foundation.

If you don't find what you need in one place, look someplace else. The answers are out there, and you will be amazed at all the resources you will find when you start looking.

You may know a lot about quilting, supplies, and exactly what you want to sell, but whatever you do, don't neglect the business end of your company. That could be disastrous. You need to know how to manage your money, keep track of your finances for the Internal Revenue Service, and spend your money to get the most out of it for your business. When you need to know about writing a business plan; finding, hiring, and firing employees; and getting the word out about your business, you can consult this book.

Learning about running a business and then growing that business never ends; it isn't a nine-to-five job. You need to stay on top of all the government regulations (federal, state, and local) that might affect your business. By learning all you can about business, you can prepare for the changes that will help your business survive and grow.

02

Getting a Clear View of Your Business

You've no doubt thought about owning and running your own business for a long time in general terms, but in this chapter let's explore the particulars. Do you want to start your business from scratch, or do you want to buy an established business? Do you want to fly solo, or have you been talking to a friend and thinking about operating as a partnership? Maybe you have a silent partner who wants to invest money but doesn't want to be involved in the day-to-day running of the business? Whichever way you go, remember that your decisions will have ramifications in your business—some for the good, some for the bad. So think carefully, ask questions, and be cautious yet firm when you make those decisions.

Investing in an Established Business

If you are thinking about buying an established quilting business, there are quite a few factors you need to think about. As in any business, there will be pros and cons. Your job is to decide whether or not the pros outweigh the cons. Don't hesitate to sit down and write these out so that you can see in black and white if this is the way you want to go. Be sure to include the following in your considerations.

Reputation

First and foremost, what kind of reputation does the business have? Are the customers loyal? If the business has a good reputation, do you have the integrity to keep up that reputation? If the current business has a bad reputation, be forewarned that it may take you a while to build your customer/client base and win back the customers who were treated badly.

How has the current owner treated employees, if any, and how have customers been treated? Has he or she dealt with problems in the business and with customers in a professional, timely, and ethical manner? If the owner does have part-time or full-time employees, has he or she paid them on time? Are they loyal to the owner and the business, or do they slack off on the job?

Knowing the backbone of the business will benefit you when it comes time for you to decide whether or not to buy. If you don't know much about the business, ask around. Customers, employees, and other people who are in the quilting arena will have an opinion. Do not take their opinions lightly. Think carefully about what others say before making your decision.

Volume

Second, is this the type of business you are interested in starting? How is its volume? Is business steady through the year, or are there downtimes? You don't want to buy a business that is stagnant. Sales volumes and orders may vary from season to season, but if the business is consistently causing the owner to struggle to survive or is currently on a downhill slide, it would be wiser for you to move on and search somewhere else.

Ask about getting the business's customer list. If you do decide to buy the business, you will want to get in touch with the old customers and invite them to come to an open house to meet you and hear about your vision. This is a good way to break the ice and start building your own customer loyalty.

Equipment

Third, if you are buying a business with sewing and quilting machines, what kind of condition are those machines in? How old are they? Are they still operational, and, if so, when were they last serviced? Check to see if the owner has a maintenance log. Do the machines have all their parts? If you buy a machine that embroiders and you don't have the attachments, it's not going to do you much good. You don't want to pay for something you don't have. The cost of buying extra parts or replacing missing pieces could add up quickly.

> **Patchwork**
>
> Have the owner write down a list of machines the business has, how much they cost, when they were purchased, any attachments the machines may have, when they were last serviced (and by whom), and the phone number of the servicing company. This is good operating sense, and it will help you in many ways. You will know how many machines are available and when they were bought. If you decide to buy the business, you will already have a list of contacts you can call if something should go wrong. This will be a huge time-saver for you.

Finances

Fourth, take a look at the financial books. If they don't make any sense to you, take them to your accountant or have an independent auditor look at them. You need to know how many liabilities the business has as well as how many assets. By getting a third party involved, you will have an unbiased opinion on the status of the business. Remember, people can tell you that they are making money, but if the books say they aren't, then you'd better steer clear. You don't want to buy a business that is financially unstable or deeply in debt.

If the owner is hesitant about showing you the financials, be hesitant about buying that business.

Legal

Finally, check to see if there are any outstanding court judgments against the business. This could be business death to you before you've even had the opportunity to get started. Liens against the business would put a legal hold on anything you might try to do, such as expand, add a quilting machine, or even move. You want to be able to do what you want with the business without being held back. Has someone tried to sue the business for some injury, real or imagined? The current owner may tell you that everything is resolved. It may be, but it is your responsibility to find out for sure.

Have there been complaints filed against this company through the Better Business Bureau. You don't want to buy a business that has had problems with customer service and its reputation. It is simple to find out. Just call the Better Business Bureau and ask.

Starting from Scratch

If you are going to start your business from scratch and have a job, you might want to keep that job for a while, unless you have someone who can pay your mortgage and feed you while you are building your clientele. You will need to think of how many quilting projects you have lined up, how much money they will bring in, and when. A good rule of thumb is to have at least three to four months' worth of projects lined up before you even consider quitting your full time job. However, if you have a partner who is taking care of the financial end of things, by all means move ahead. Just know in advance that it will take a while for you to earn a profit.

Another thing to consider is that even though you have a list of projects, you will need to continue looking for prospective clients and customers. You will need to talk about your business and pass out your business cards all the time—weekdays, week-nights, and weekends. This isn't a nine-to-five job anymore; this is your business, and you need to work at it full-time, at least until you get your name out there.

Now, are you looking to grow or do you want to stay small? Now is the time to be planning what you need to do to accomplish either of these goals. If your goal is to expand your business and hire employees, think about how you can accomplish it. If you plan to stay small and be a one-man show, remember that when you aren't working on the business, you aren't making money. We'll talk more about this in chapter 9.

Have you thought about your dreams and goals for your business? This is the point where you'll want to do so. Sit down and write a statement of where you want your business to be in one year, five years, and ten years. Your statement doesn't have to be more than a sentence. The purpose of this exercise is to develop a clear vision of where you want your business to go and what you want it to achieve. As the old saying goes, "You'll never hit a target if you don't aim for one."

Going It Alone versus Adding a Partner

Running your own business is a big responsibility. When you operate it by yourself, you and you alone make the decisions for the business: what jobs you will accept, how the work is done, and where the money will be channeled when the work is complete. When you take on a partner, you will need to get an OK on everything you do.

Right now, you may expect that in a partnership, both partners will do the same amount of work. Be aware however, that in partnerships the workload can often become uneven. In some, one partner will get all the orders, work on the projects, answer the phone, collect the money, and do everything else. This can wear a partnership thin. One partner will feel overworked while the other may be making the same amount of money doing nothing. In this case you are better off having an employee instead of a partner.

"But my friend and I have been talking about this for a long time," you may say. A word of caution: A business is the best way to ruin a friendship. You both need to sit down and discuss your expectations to make sure you both have the same vision for the business.

If you feel you need to take on a partner because there is some aspect of the business you are apprehensive about, sit down and write out what you feel is lacking. Take a good, hard look and decide whether a partner would benefit or hinder your plans and goals. You can always learn what you need to know as you grow your business.

The following short quiz might help you decide if a partnership would be right for you or if it would be more trouble than it's worth:

1. **Is your potential business partner a friend?** It's one thing to see your friend once or twice a week, but every day could be too much. While you may love this person, you need to admit now if there are things about your friend that annoy you. Your slight irritations could be greatly amplified if you go into business together. Think of partnering with a friend in business as a marriage. Are you willing to be with this person every day, at the very least five days a week, for ten to twelve hours or more?

2. **How long have you known this person?** This may seem like an easy and logical question, but if you haven't considered it, you need to. Most people wouldn't marry someone they just met yesterday. You need to use the same caution when choosing a business partner. "I've known Mary for almost a year now," you may say. That's not long enough. A good rule of thumb is to have known the person at least five years, and even that may not be long enough. Five years, however, is a good gauge of whether your potential partner is a stable, stay-in-one-place, consistent person or one who gets bored and drifts.

3. **Is this person reliable, trustworthy, and hardworking?** When your friend promises to do something, can you believe it? If you left on vacation, could

you trust your partner to run your business without stealing from it? Would you worry about your business while you were gone? Is your friend willing to jump right in and do whatever the business requires? Is your potential partner willing to stay late or come in early to get a job done or an order out? If you answered no to any of these questions, rethink your choice of partner.

4. **What applicable skills will your partner bring to the business?** Maybe you aren't good with numbers and your partner is a whiz? Maybe your partner knows how to do bookkeeping, or perhaps design patterns to sell through your business, something you've never mastered. If you are going to take on a partner, that partner needs to bring something to the business that will benefit it. If not, why give share half your profits?

5. **What is this person's view on being a business owner?** Is your friend aware of how much work is involved? Sure, he or she may think it would be great to own a business with someone else, but owning that business does not mean you can take off whenever you want or do whatever you want. Is your potential partner willing to work as hard as you are to make a go of it? If you want to grow your business and your friend wants to stay small, perhaps this isn't the partner for you.

6. **Is this person successful?** By success I don't mean running a multimillion-dollar company or winning major awards in the community. I mean the success of having friends, the respect of the community, a good home and family life, and, a generally upbeat and self-confident manner.

7. **Is your friend an optimist or a pessimist?** You do not want to partner with someone who is going to continually drag you down with negativity and complaints about everything from the weather to the way someone walks. Working day after day with someone who is a drag can make the days long and uncomfortable. It's a proven fact when you are subjected to negativity on a daily basis, you begin to think that way too. You don't need that kind of attitude when starting your business.

8. **Does your potential partner have the same work ethic you do?** If given a job to complete, will this person produce the same quality work you would? Will your friend give your customers the same customer service you would and treat them with the respect? Does your friend take pride in a job well done?

9. **What kind of image does this person project?** Think about how this person looks to others. Do they see a neat, moderate dresser or someone who is generously tattoed, pierced, or garbed in garish, unconventional clothing? While there is a lot to be said for individuality, you don't want to scare away potential customers, either. Also, if your friend cusses like a sailor or throws emotional hissy fits, you might think twice about taking on this person as your partner. When clients or customers come to you, you want them to feel comfortable talking to you and your partner on the phone or face to face.

10. **What kind of personality does your potential partner have?** Is this person easygoing, or does your friend fly off the handle at each little problem? Watch out for a temperament that's impulsive, aloof, or pushy. You don't want a partner who makes rash decisions that might hurt the business, or one who either ignores customers or alienates them with high-pressure tactics. Your partner should complement your personality and be as motivated as you are about building your business.

If, after you have thought about and answered the above questions, you decide to take on a partner, you need to find an attorney to draw up a partnership agreement. While it may cost you a little bit of money, it is important because it will protect your business and protect you. In this agreement, you will need to include what percentage of the business each partner will own and what specific duties each partner will perform. You will also need to decide and include how much of the business each partner will get if the business is dissolved for any reason. If your potential partner doesn't want to sign or be a part of the agreement, think twice about going through with the partnership. You might also consider working together for three to six months in the actual business setting in order to judge temperament compatibility and how you like the working situation.

While it may seem that we've been concentrating on the negatives, there are some plus sides to having a partner. In the end, a partner shares the financial burden, helps in assessing new ideas and solving problems, and helps you carry the workload when it gets busy. That's the easy part of having a business partner.

How Do You Want to Run Your Business?

Now that you have decided on your business, you need to think about the tax and legal ramifications of the four business types—corporation, partnership, LLC, or sole proprietorship. You will want to sit down and talk with an attorney and your accountant to discuss your options and make sure you are choosing the correct type for your business. Choosing one type over another could mean the difference between your paying one thousand or ten thousand dollars a year in taxes. Let's take a look at each business type and their advantages and disadvantages.

Sole Proprietorship

A *sole proprietorship* is the oldest, most common, easiest, and least expensive type of business to set up. As the name implies, a single person owns and operates this kind of business. To make it clearer, the Internal Revenue Service defines a sole proprietor as someone who owns an unincorporated business alone.

On the downside, you and you alone take all the risks. You are responsible for checking with state and local authorities to secure any required permits, business licenses, and registrations for your business. As the business owner, you are responsible for any taxes and debt, and you are personally liable for any vendor fraud, lawsuits, or default on loans. This means that if for some reason your business went belly up financially and you had outstanding debts, creditors could come in and take your possessions, including your equipment, inventory, cars, paintings, and even your house if the business debt is large enough. Because you are considered self-employed as a sole proprietor by the government, you can't collect unemployment or worker's compensation.

On the plus side, though, you control your own fate. You are the boss, you have complete control over all matters of your business, and you reap all the profits. From a legal and tax standpoint, you and the business are one.

If you want to be a sole proprietorship, you really don't have to do anything. If you don't incorporate, become an LLC, or take on a partner, you are automatically considered a sole proprietorship business.

Because this is to be a home-based quilting business, this is probably the way you will want to go when you first start out. First, this type of business is easy to set up and dissolve. Second, when you die, the business dies. As long as you run the business out of your home and have only a limited number of employees, a sole proprietorship is probably the easiest and most affordable option for you.

Partnership

A *partnership* occurs when you and a partner—a friend, relative, associate, or group of partners—go into business together. Each partner brings a unique set of skills, expertise, and money to the business in exchange for a portion of the business's profits. All you need to set up a partnership is a partnership agreement, which is fairly simple. Find an attorney to draw one up and then have all interested parties sign it. This agreement is important and should be a priority, as you want to protect yourself and your business.

When entering into such an agreement, all partners are recognized as legal owners. Each partner can make decisions for the business, hire and fire employees, operate the business, and borrow money on the business's behalf. Each partner is taxed on his share of the business profits, and each is personally responsible for debts and taxes incurred by the business.

While there are pros to having a partner—like having someone to bounce ideas off of, to share expenses and work hours with, and to delegate tasks to when you may not be able to or want to do them—there are cons as well. Probably the biggest con is that each partner is legally responsible and accountable for what the other partner does in the business. For example, if you have a partner who is irresponsible with money, hires questionable employees, or operates the business in an unprofessional manner, that behavior will reflect on you. You can also run into problems if you or your partner makes business decisions the other one disagrees with. What if your partner takes on jobs that you are ill equipped to handle, and as a result you turn out a shoddy product? Maybe your partner is mad because you are both making the same amount, but he or she is doing most of the work. What if your partner thinks you should scale back but you want to expand? These situations can turn ugly quickly and destroy not only a business, but a friendship.

Limited Partnership

To lessen negative impacts like these, you might want to consider a *limited partnership*. In a limited partnership, one partner makes the day-to-day operating decisions and the other, the limited partner, exercises limited involvement but is a source of capital or money. The pros of this type of partnership are that you will have capital if you need it and have someone to bounce ideas off. The cons are that the general partner is fully liable if there are legal problems or if the company fails. The limited partner is shielded from liabilities because he or she did not participate in the daily operation of the business. You will also need to get this partner's approval if you want to change your role in the business or take on another partner, perhaps one who will be more involved in the business. For this type of partnership, you must register with each partner's state, and a franchise tax is required to file certification.

Remember, secure an attorney to assist you in setting up all partnership agreements, whether they are full or limited. Make sure everything is discussed and written down in black and white. Any questions you have need to be answered and settled before you sign on the dotted line. The price of an attorney is a small fee to pay now compared to what you may have to pay if legal issues arise in the future.

Corporation

Another option you have is to set up your business as a *corporation*. The Small Business Administration defines a corporation as "a legal entity separate from its owners, who own shares of stock in its company." So being a legal separate entity, a corporation has its own set of liabilities, rights, and privileges apart from its owner.

There are downsides, however, to organizing your business this way. Corporations are difficult to create and can be complex. The government imposes stricter regulations on corporations than on any other business type. You will need to do state filings when your business is created, and you will have to continue paying state filings and fees as long as the corporation is in existence. Your business as a corporation will have to elect directors and officers (i.e., president, vice president, secretary, and treasurer), hold annual board meetings, keep monthly minutes, and issue stock certificates.

The pros of having a corporation are that it projects a good business image, has limited liability protection, and typically can raise capital easier than other kinds of businesses.

C Corporations versus S Corporations

If you are considering going the corporation route, be sure to talk to your accountant about the two types: a C Corporation and a Subchapter S Corporation.

A C Corporation is a beast unto itself. It must hold to all the strict government regulations and licensing of a corporation, and it is taxed double, first at the corporate level and then again through the stockholders' dividends.

A Subchapter S Corporation is like the C in many ways except in taxation. If a company qualifies for S status, the corporation is taxed like a partnership or a sole proprietorship. This means that your business will be taxed at an individual rate rather than a corporate one.

Many small businesses go with a Subchapter S Corporation because they like the separation of the business from their personal liabilities and assets. While the taxes are a bit higher than for a sole proprietorship, some feel it's worth it for the security.

You or your tax accountant can contact the Internal Revenue Service to see if you qualify for S Corporation status. You can also request IRS Pamphlet 589 to get an overview of S Corporation requirements to see if you qualify before contacting your accountant. It would be a good business practice to request this information from the IRS every other year. Government rules and regulations change almost every year and swiftly, so you don't want to be caught by surprise fees or fines because you didn't know about those changes.

If you decide to expand your business and move from your home to an office building, you will probably want to think more seriously about becoming an S Corporation. Talk to your accountant, who will be the best person to tell you about taxes and fees involved when changing.

Limited Liability Company (LLC)

The final business type is a *limited liability company,* or LLC. It is a fairly new legal business designation that is designed to allow "management flexibility" the way a general partnership does but provide the limited liability of a corporation.

Although requirements and regulations may change from state to state, an LLC is recognized in all fifty states. Owners are known as members, and when forming an LLC, those members are required to file organizational articles with their state's secretary of state. Each member must also submit an operating agreement stating what the relationship is between the member and any other members, and the company.

The pros of an LLC are that the paperwork for organizing and maintaining this form of business costs less than maintaining a corporation, you pay federal taxes as though you were a partnership, and members have limited personal liability.

The cons are that some states require an LLC to operate with more than one person, it costs more to set up than a sole proprietorship, and the company dissolves when the owner entity dies.

	PROS	CONS
Sole Proprietorship	Owner is his or her own boss. Owner makes all the profits. Easy to set up.	Owner takes all the risk. Owner is responsible for everything that happens in the company—good or bad.
Partnership	Have someone to bounce ideas off of. Someone to share the good and bad. Someone to help with the workload and fill in where you might be lacking.	You are responsible for what your partner does and doesn't do. You share profits with your partner. Takes a little more work to set up.
Corporation	Projects good business image. Limited liability protection. Can raise capital more easily.	Difficult to set up. Government has tighter regulations and restrictions. Have to hold meetings, keep minutes, and issue stock.
Limited Liability Company	Costs less than a corporation to set up. Pay federal tax at the partnership rate rather than the corporation rate. Limited personal liability.	In most states, must have more than one person. Costs more to set up than a sole proprietorship. Company dissolves when the owner entity dies.

Look at all these business types carefully and figure out which one will benefit your business the most. You don't want to have to pay a lot of taxes or be bogged down with so much paperwork that you can't run your business, yet you need to protect yourself. By speaking to an attorney and accountant, you should be able to figure out the best way to go for your particular needs.

03

Necessary Quilting Equipment

Perhaps you have already collected quite a number of the tools and machines you will be using for your business. If you have been making quilts and selling them, chances are you already own many of the items we will be talking about in this chapter. As you look through the list, you might find one or two that will enhance your business. You don't have to own everything mentioned here. Buy what you will use and what will work for you. We will also be covering what you might want to purchase for running a home office in the next chapter, as that will be an important part of your business as well.

Investing in Quilting Tools and Equipment

As you start buying your scissors, material, and machines, remember to buy quality products. Typically, high-quality equipment isn't much more expensive than the cheaper brands. You will be using your equipment and many of your tools every day, so you want them to be durable. My grandmother had a metal pair of scissors she used to cut out all her patterns. When she died, the scissors were passed down to me. Over the years, I have purchased numerous other pairs of scissors, but none have stayed as sharp or held up as well as hers. Granted, her scissors had only been used to cut patterns from fabric, but some of the scissors currently being sold wouldn't even cut through ten sets of patterns let alone cut for ten years and still remain sharp. I can only remember my grandfather sharpening them once.

This list is organized from the least expensive overall to the most expensive. Some items can be very expensive, but others you can acquire for a nominal fee. Check around at different stores and online. In some instances you can find great prices and sales at different times of the year. You will find that some items work better for you than others. Ask others what works for them and go from there.

Marking Pencil or Fabric Chalk

You might want to think about investing in one or two marking pencils, commonly known as tailor's pencils. When you need to make a seam a certain way or just get a line straight, you can draw on your fabric and then brush or wash it off. There are three recommended products in the sewing world. The first is the Dritz Dual Purpose Marking Pen. One end is purple disappearing ink and the other is blue. Second is the Clover Chaco Lined Pen, which is refillable. Third is the Fons & Porter White Mechanical Fabric Pencil, which is refillable as well. If you are working with delicate patterns, this pencil draws fine lines and may help you stay within the confines of your pattern. Prices range from five to fifteen dollars.

Needle Threader

You may not need one of these right away, but one never knows. They typically come at a nominal cost, and if you need one even once, you will wish you had forked out the four to ten dollars to buy one. These small tools help you put thread through the eye of a needle, small or otherwise. You can buy a small, flimsy Dritz needle threader for around four dollars or a heavy-duty one for around eight to twelve dollars.

Seam Ripper

Mistakes happen. Seams slip and get sewn crooked, or the wrong piece gets sewn to the wrong piece. While you could use a needle to rip out the thread, a seam ripper is much more efficient. There are still the traditional rippers, but you might want to invest in an ergonomic one if you have hand pain or a lighted seam ripper if your eyes are bad, you have poor light, or you tend to work with dark fabric. Seam rippers can range in price from four to twenty dollars.

Quilting Pins

You no doubt have these already, but if you don't, make sure to stock up. Quilting pins have either little balls on the top or flat flower heads, and they are made of stainless steel. Make sure you purchase stainless steel, as you don't want the pins to rust over time. Most quilting pins come sharp and super fine, which helps them through multiple layers of fabric. Dritz and Clover seem to be the most popular brands. Prices range from nine to thirteen dollars and packages tend to range from one hundred to one thousand pins.

To the Point

- Invest in a magnetic pinholder if you haven't already. These little gems can be lifesavers when you are involved in a project and accidentally knock your pins off the table. A magnetic pinholder keeps them together. There are many different types and brands, with prices ranging from five to twenty dollars.

- If a pin seems to be getting dull, you don't have to throw it away or run out and buy a new package. Run the pin through your hair, next to your scalp. The oil on your head will sharpen the point.

- Keep your pins and needles sharp by periodically sticking them in soap. This coats your pins so they slide through fabric without your having to force them.

Quilting Curved Safety Pins

You may not need to purchase these pins at first, but perhaps invest in a package after a few quilt sales. The safety pins are curved so that you can easily slip them under all your fabric layers, secure the material, and baste as needed. The pins come in sizes 0 to 4 and are made out of nickel-plated brass so that they won't rust or tarnish, thus ruining your quilt. This is a purchase where quality is important. Some of the cheaper curved pins are made out of thin metal and have been known to break when put through the thicker fabrics. Check out manufacturers like Bohin, Dritz, Collins, and Fons & Porter for quality.

Quilting Needles

You probably have some of these in your sewing basket already, but if you don't, you might want to make an investment. These needles are shorter than regular sewing needles and have smaller eyes. They allow you to get through layers of fabric more easily and to pull up threads without too much effort. They can be found almost anywhere sewing supplies are sold and range in price from three to five dollars a package.

Scissors

Owning a good pair of scissors is essential when it comes to cutting materials for a long period. You probably already own a pair that you are fond of, but if not, now is the time to invest. The best approach is to find one that fits comfortably in your hand and that cuts easily and evenly. Fiskars and Gingher seem to be the two top brands for quilters. Their scissors range in size from four inches to nine and a half inches and can cost anywhere from five to fifty dollars. Havel's is another popular brand. Victoria Findlay Wolfe, a quilter from New York, says she likes her Havel's because they always stay sharp.

Another scissors investment is a pair of pinking shears, the scissors whose blades have teeth. These can save you hours of headaches by allowing you to cut cotton materials without having them unravel on you. A good pair can cost you about fifty dollars, but once you make the investment, they should last a lifetime.

Cutting Mat

If you haven't invested in a cutting mat, now is the time. Quilters swear by them. Because you are going into the business of quilting, this is one of the must-have items in your arsenal. Cutting mats allow you to take a pattern and material and cut several layers of that pattern at once. You can cut faster and get more done with the mat.

The mats come in all sizes, ranging from six inches by six inches to thirty-six inches by forty-eight inches. One quilter found a mat the size of her cutting table, so oversize mats are available if you know where to look. Some cutting mats are gridded, which allows you to line up a piece of material with a ruler and cut away. There are also non-gridded mats for those who would rather work without the distraction of lines.

Check into the self-healing mats. After cutting through materials into these mats, they fill in where the cuts are made and become smooth so you don't have deep grooves next time you cut out another pattern. They will run you a little more in price, but are worth it in the long run. Depending on what size and brand you buy, a cutting mat can cost you between ten and forty dollars. The more popular brands among quilters are Fiskars, Olfa, Omnigrid, X-ACTO, and Uline.

Rotary Cutters

After you invest in a good cutting mat, you'll want to find a quality rotary cutter to use with it. These might be described as rotary scissors, as they will help you cut through fabric and save you time by cutting through multiple layers. As with the mats, there are several brands to choose from. Olfa, Fiskars, and Gingher seem to be the most popular. You can find rotary cutters with straight or ergonomic handles. They range in price from eight to seventy dollars, depending on the brand. Remember, these tools are an investment. While you certainly don't need to buy the most expensive one out there, if you invest in a good cutter, it will last you a long time.

Because you will be using your cutter regularly, especially if you plan on cutting "fat squares" to sell, the blade on your cutter will eventually become dull and you will need to trade out blades or sharpen them. There are blade sharpeners available on the market that range in size and price. If your blade becomes dull rather quickly, you might want to consider investing in a sharpener. These range in price from twenty to forty dollars and are substantially cheaper in the long run than buying new blades every time yours get dull.

Rulers

When thinking about acquiring work tools for your business, don't overlook the clear acrylic quilting rulers. These handy implements come in all sizes and shapes. They can be rectangular, L-shaped, triangular, circular, or square. They are clear and marked with a two-color grid (typically black and red) that makes for easy reading. Because these rulers are made out of hard plastic, they make following straight lines a breeze. As with all quilting supplies, there are many brands available, but a few stand out from the others. Omnigrid is at the top of the list, with Creative Grid and EZ Quilt tying for a close second. Most quilters own several different sizes. Quilting rulers can range in price from fourteen to sixty dollars, depending on what size and shape you choose.

Beyond Design

"My all-time favorite tool is the rotary cutter," Betty Hairfield of Betsy's Quilts in Oklahoma says. "I can cut a complete quilt top in two to three hours. It is so much better than using scissors."

Thread

You will need a good supply of thread. You probably already have a pretty good stash on hand. If not, now is the time to start building up that stash. Most quilters use 100 percent cotton thread for their quilts' construction, but don't overlook the silk and wool threads available. You will also want to keep an eye out for specialty threads that can add accent colors to your quilts. Of course, brown, white, and black are the most commonly used, but don't overlook hot pinks, spring greens, and any other color you might find on sale. You never know when you might need different colors. A good way to build up your stash is to look for sales on thread. If you already know what colors you use the most, concentrate on those, but if not and you can find a spool for 50 to 80 percent off the regular price, stock up.

A caution when buying thread: Make sure it is not too old. A good way to test thread to see if it will work for you is to try to break it. If it breaks easily, don't buy it. Nothing is more frustrating than a quilt not staying together because your thread is weak. Popular brands include Aurifil, Gutermann, Clover, and Coats & Clark.

Patchwork

If you are looking to spice up some of your quilt pieces, specialty threads like Robison Anton Solar Active Color Changing Thread might provide just the pizzazz you are looking for. These threads look one color when out of the sunlight and change to another when in the sunlight. Check them out at robison-anton.com.

Fabric

As with thread, you will want an ample fabric supply. No doubt you already own closets full of it, but in the quilting business, as multiple quilters have told me, "one can never have too much fabric." Start out collecting cotton, the easiest material to sew. However, don't hesitate to collect flannel, lace, and silk. One quilter purchased boxes of silk ties from a manufacturer who was going out of business to make her silk kaleidoscope quilts. Now she has plenty of silk and will be able to work with many different colors and patterns. When starting up, ask around to family members and friends who sew. They will probably have boxes of scraps you can add to your stash. You never know what treasures you can find among the scraps other people are ready to throw out.

Lighting

Most people may not think a light beyond what's overhead would be important, but most quilters say having a light directly over the cutting table or sewing machine can be a lifesaver. If you don't get much natural light from windows, think about investing in a floor or table lamp. These can be positioned where you need them, when you need them.

Sewing dark materials with dark thread or ripping out seams can cause severe eyestrain if you don't have a good light. Also, even if you do have plenty of windows for light, it does get dark eventually, and a single overhead light at night may not be enough illumination if you are working on a tedious project. OttLites seem to be the most popular. They range in price from $30 to $250, depending on the style you choose. Watch for sales as they come around quite often.

Ironing Board and Iron

If you don't own these items now, you should invest in them right away. They are essential not only for helping you make quilts, but also for pressing the seams together correctly. After you sew, you will need to press the seams down, especially if you are making a multifaceted quilt. You will need a steam iron to make sure the seams lie flat.

Black & Decker makes a nice steam iron for around fifty dollars. Panasonic and Rowenta also offer irons at comparable prices. If you are looking for a cut above, check in to the Oliso irons. Their smart models automatically turn off and have iTouch technology, which means that when your hand is off the handle, the iron raises so your material will not scorch or burn. These irons are more expensive, starting at eighty dollars, but if you have the money, it would be a good investment.

Choose an ironing board that will hit you at hip level. You want it to be a comfortable height so that you aren't bending over all the time. A wall unit is ideal if you have the space. Wall units can range from $99 to $300. Freestanding units are much cheaper.

Don't forget about padding and a cover. While your board may come with a foam pad, a felt pad will hold its shape better in the long run, so you might try to find one of those. A Teflon-coated cotton cover won't stick to your fabrics and is easy to clean.

Worktable

Ask any quilter and every one will tell you that a worktable is crucial. As one quilter said when asked about reasons for a worktable, "Let me count the ways." You will use your worktable to cut your designs, lay them out, pin, and keep all your pieces together. You'll be going back to your worktable over and over again.

Finding a worktable will not be difficult. Quilters use everything from old dining room tables to office conference tables depending on what's available and if the price is right. Keep in mind a couple of things when deciding on yours:

- Make sure it has a smooth top and edges. You don't want anything that will snag or tear your fabric.
- Check the height of the table. You don't want to have to bend over so much that it hurts your back, but you don't want it to be so high that your shoulders get tired. An adjustable table is ideal.
- Get a table that will fit in your workspace, yet is big enough for your needs. Measure, measure, measure. Know how large a space you have before you fill it with a table. You want to have room to move around it. With that said, you want to have a big enough table so you can spread out. Worktables can be round, square, or rectangular. Rectangular tables can range anywhere from four to six feet long.

Remember, get what works best for you.

Sewing Machine

Quilters who have been in the business for a long time will tell you they own more than one sewing machine. They may have the first sewing machine they started with, an embroidery machine, and one that is the quilting workhorse. While the average is three, some quilters own five or six, not including their longarm and midarm quilting machines. While that seems to be the norm, you certainly don't have to have three or more machines to start your business. One will be sufficient. The key is to find one that suits you and will do what you want it to do.

In her book, *Quilter's Review Guide to Finding a Sewing Machine You'll Love*, Sharon Darling echoes that advice: "My advice is to buy the best machine you can possibly afford." And by best machines, she means that there are certain criteria to look for in a quilting sewing machine:

1. **Look for a machine that makes a consistent, even stitch.** Bernina makes a machine with a stitch regulator. Other companies have tried to emulate the device, but because Bernina was the pioneer, most sewers refer to the Bernina brand.

2. **Look for a sturdy machine.** There are still heavy-duty machines out there that will last you years and through hundreds of hours of sewing. Remember, you will be sewing through several layers of fabric and sometimes batting. You want a machine that will stand up to the rigors of what you throw at it.

3. **Consider investing in a machine that has a fabric feeder on the top and bottom.** Quilters say these are great when you have to sew through many layers. Along the same line, make sure your sewing pressure foot can handle multiple layers and that there is enough space to get multiple layers under the foot as you prepare to sew.

4. **Try to get a machine with a sewing table extension.** (Some people call this a table extension arm.) This is the platform you will place your material on as you sew. Just as a sleeve extension allows you to slip a cuff over the sewing arm and sew evenly, a table extension will allow you more space when you are sewing large quilt sections together.

5. **Check out the control pedals.** Some machines have knee controls that drive your material. Other machines have floor pedals. There are also machines that have pedal-operated forward and reverse.

While there are many different brand names available, those most frequently bandied around by quilters are Pfaff, Bernina, Husqvarna Viking, Janome, Brother, Baby Lock, Elna, Juki, and Swedish Innovation, to name only a few. The kind of machine you get will depend on your budget and what you prefer. Sewing machines can range from four to three thousand dollars.

Today, quilting drives the sewing machine business, and manufacturers know it. There are exclusive perks and offers for those who are looking to purchase. Below are a few pieces of advice when starting your search:

1. **Test-drive several different types of machines.** This will help you get a feel for how a machine sews and how comfortable you are with it. A good place to find many different machines at once is at quilt and/or sewing shows or exhibitions. Check with your local quilt guild or go online and type "quilt show" or "sewing exhibition" into a search engine. You will find hundreds of these shows across the country, so there is sure to be one located near you. Don't be shy. Try out as many different machines as you can. Ask questions, and when the salesmen tell you about their offers, take the information, but don't make a rash decision.

2. **Check out dealers in your local area.** If you find a machine you like at a particular trade show, see if there is a dealer near you. If so, go in and talk to the dealership. Most of these stores offer maintenance, classes, and tools you can buy to improve the efficiency of your machine. Also, if you buy from a dealer, he can tell you what is and is not included in your warranty. Dealers may also be able to work with you if you need financing or want to put a machine on layaway.

3. **Don't neglect trade-ins.** There are two ways this can work. If you become acquainted with a dealer and you buy your machine from him, you may be able to trade in your current name brand when a newer model becomes available and get a great deal. Quilters say it's the same concept as trading in a car. Conversely, you may be able to buy a slightly older model that has been traded in for a great price. Ask dealers about their trade-in policies—or perhaps I should say their trade-*up* policies.

4. **Talk to fellow quilters.** Ask why they bought the specific machines they purchased and if you can test drive their favorite. They will tell you what they like about their machines and why they like them.

Patchwork

When buying a sewing machine, don't forget to buy extra needles and ask about different attachments. You might want to get several different walking foots or, at the very least, see what is available in case you need to expand in the future. Extras are a big part of buying a machine, so don't hesitate to ask and take the seller up on any special offers.

Quilting Machines

Let me start off by saying you certainly don't need a longarm or even a midarm quilting machine to start a quilting business, but a lot of money can be made if you do own one of these machines, so they had to be included in this chapter.

Longarm and midarm quilting machines are what home-based business owners use to actually quilt the quilt tops once the tops are sewn together.

Longarm Quilting Machine

While you can quilt on a sewing machine or by hand, a longarm quilting machine makes the task easier, faster, and so much more efficient. Using a longarm machine, you mount the quilt with your three layers (top, batting, backing) on rollers. Then you guide the machine as it sews across the quilt at various stages.

If you are thinking about purchasing a longarm quilting machine, make sure you have plenty of space. Typical longarm tables run anywhere from eight to fourteen feet long, and the width can range from four feet to eight feet. Once the equipment is installed, you will need at least three feet around the table to navigate.

The top three manufacturers of longarm machines are Gammill Quilting Systems, American Professional Quilting Systems, and Nolting Manufacturing. The machines range in price from five thousand dollars used to twenty thousand dollars new. Add on computerized programming and your investment could soar as high as thirty-five thousand dollars. If you plan on finishing quilts for a lot of clients, then the longarm machine may be the best way to go.

Midarm Quilting Machine

If you are quilting on a smaller scale, making projects for yourself and maybe finishing a quilt or two a year for clients, you might be better served with a midarm quilting machine. Midarm machines are lighter, slightly smaller than their longarm cousins, and can cost anywhere from a half to a third of what longarms cost—typically from four to nine thousand dollars. Top midarm manufacturers are Nolting Manufacturing, which makes the Fun Quilter (funquilter.com); Handi Quilter (handiquilter.com); and Hinterberg Designs (hinterberg.com), which makes the Voyager 17.

Now, you certainly don't need one of these machines to start a business, but home-based business quilters who do own these and finish quilts for clients make good money. They are kept quite busy, sometimes having a backlog of one to two months. If you don't have one of these machines now, perhaps it would be a goal for you to set for the future, if you ever wanted to expand your business or branch out into the finishing arena.

As with sewing machines, make sure you ask around and test-drive any machine you may be thinking about purchasing. Read reviews, visit a dealership in your area, or, if possible, visit the manufacturer directly. Ask questions and be sure what you are purchasing is right for you. These machines are a big investment.

Quilt Design Program

If you want to go into quilt design, you might want to consider purchasing some computer programs. While these are certainly not essential when first starting your business, they may be something you'll want to purchase later on. There are many programs on the market, from advanced quilting techniques to creating and designing quilt patterns to computerized programs that will run your longarm and midarm quilting machines.

If you are looking to learn advanced quilting techniques, do a Google search for "quilting techniques." Your search will produce hundreds of DVD classes and online live-streaming classes. Be sure to read the reviews for these programs, as some may be better suited for you than others.

Two of the top programs that allow you to create, design, save, and print your own traditional quilt patterns are Electric Quilt 7 (aka EQ7) and Perfect Quilt. Electric Quilt 7 is sold by Electric Quilt and costs around $190. As of this writing, you can still purchase EQ6 for $150 and then upgrade to EQ7. If you have EQ5 or EQ6 already, you might want to look into the upgrade anyway. They are always coming out with new bells and whistles to make quilting more exciting. Perfect Quilt is sold by softexpressions .com and costs about $140. It is the brainchild of quilting software guru Jenny Haskins. On Soft Expressions websites, you can see pages about how the program is designed and read reviews from other customers.

Finally, there are also computerized attachment programs designed for quilting machines. If you buy a longarm or midarm machine, contact the manufacturer and ask which program works best for the machine you have. While most quilting

> **Patchwork**
>
> An excellent organizational tool to get you started is a two-drawer file cabinet. One drawer can hold your patterns and owner's manuals for your machines, while the other drawer can hold client lists and other information. As your business grows, you can buy a four-drawer cabinet and use the same concept. You can then slide the two-drawer under your worktable or desk and use it for inactive client files, tax records, and anything else you don't need daily.

finishers use pantographs (quilting patterns on paper) or free-form quilt finishing, computer programs allow the user to hook up longarm machines and program them so that the job becomes automated.

Other equipment you will need is a computer, printer/copier/fax machine, business cards, and office supplies, which we'll address in the next chapter, when we talk about setting up your office area.

Quilting Equipment Checklist

- ❏ Marking pencil or fabric chalk
- ❏ Needle threader
- ❏ Seam ripper
- ❏ Quilting pins or quilting curved safety pins
- ❏ Quilting needles
- ❏ Scissors
- ❏ Cutting mat
- ❏ Rotary cutters
- ❏ Rulers
- ❏ Thread
- ❏ Fabric
- ❏ Lighting
- ❏ Ironing board and iron
- ❏ Worktable
- ❏ Sewing machine
- ❏ Longarm or midarm quilting machine
- ❏ Quilt design program

Organizing and Maintaining Your Work Tools

Now that you have all the items you need, you may wonder what to do with them all. Fortunately, most of your work items are small. These days, there are some great organizers that can help you keep it all together, so that you know where everything is and can get to it in a matter of seconds.

As your business grows, you will acquire more items. Just remember to keep everything together and organized so you can find the things you need in a pinch. A quick word here about keeping your work supplies in good working order. While some business owners may not think about this because they now own and operate their own business, you don't want to keep dumping money into the same items over and over again.

With that said, you need to keep your work supplies in good shape. That means making sure your fabric scissors are used only for cutting fabric. It means making sure your pins and needles stay sharp. You can also buy pincushions filled with sand or make your own.

Maintenance on your sewing machine and quilting machine is a must as well. When you first purchased your machine, your owner's manual should have told you how often you need to clean out the lint from the bobbin trap or oil parts that need to be oiled. It also would have told you when you need to take the machines in for professional maintenance. Do not overlook this or put it off. It may cost you a little bit of money, but it will be well worth it in the long run. A little time spent on maintenance will keep you up and running instead of waiting for a machine part. Besides, you may be able to write off this expense on your taxes.

04 Getting Started

After reading the first three chapters, you should have a good idea of what kind of business you want to operate and the kinds of tools you need to run your business. You probably have everything you need and are ready to get started. Let's look at a few more areas, however, before you get to work and hang up your business shingle.

Choosing Your Business Name

For obvious reasons, the first thing you need to do, if you haven't done so already, is choose a business name. This is a very important step when building a business, and ample time should be given to the process. Maybe you've already thought about the name you want to use. If so, great. If you haven't, however, please do so now. Even if you have a name already, please take the time to consider the suggestions below before you start marketing your business.

First, do some research. Before you start using the first name that pops into your head, look through the phone book in the business section or hop on the Yellow Pages website to look at the names listed. You might also gather some business cards and consider what business names are already being used. Make a list of the names your competition is using and compare that list to what you are considering.

Pick a snappy name, one someone can remember—but one a person can pronounce too. It's fine if you want to use something like "Samantha's Quilts," incorporating your name into the business, especially if you want to stay small and be a one-person show. But if you have bigger plans, like expanding somewhere down the road, you might want to choose a more generic business name like "Quality Quilting" or "Special Somethings."

Names like the last two are also unlimiting, whereas Samantha's Quilts implies that all you do is make quilts. Quality Quilting can say you do more than quilts because then you can make quilted purses, pot holders, table runners, and more. You don't want to choose a name that limits your business potential.

Think about using the KISS method: Keep It Short and Sweet. You want to choose something that represents your business, but at the same time, brevity can be your best friend. You want something that will fit on a business card or in a small ad, and something that can be typed into a search engine or URL line quickly and easily. If you pick something that zings, people will remember it.

Next, check Register.com to see if your business name is taken already. One of the many things you'll want to do when building your business is build a website. We'll talk about this more in chapter 8 but for now, just make sure your business name is available. You don't want to choose a name, have business cards made, and then not be able to use the name. It's best if no one has the same business name so that you can purchase your website URL as a .com, but .net is also acceptable.

Once you have decided on a business name and have determined that it's available, run it past your family and friends for feedback. However they feel about it, ask them two questions: What kind of business does it say you do, and why do they like or dislike it? If they don't like it or can't tell what kind of business you are planning, ask for their suggestions. Then you might want to go back to the research stage.

You might want to have several options from the start so that you don't become attached to one. That way, if you need to choose another, you will be ready.

After you have chosen your business name, you may have to register it, depending on which state you live in. This can usually be done in your county clerk's office or through the state government. However, if you are a sole proprietorship or have a partner, you will probably be able to get by with a DBA ("doing business as") and just file the business under your name.

For more information on registering your business name, visit the Small Business Administration website (sba.gov) and do a search for "registering your business name."

Zoning, Licenses, and Permits

Before you move forward with any home-based business plans, check to see if you can have a home-based business and what, if any, local licenses or permits are required.

First, you will need to find out how your property is zoned. To do this, you will need to contact your local planning agency. Most county agencies, like your county clerk's office and state agencies, can tell you where you need to go to find yours. As you may know, property is zoned as residential or business. Even though you will be operating a home-based quilting business, some areas restrict any type of business operation. Period.

While overall zoning ordinances have loosened, you will still find restrictions on structural changes to your home, traffic, signage, storage, noise, odors, and perhaps other items unique to your neighborhood. If you live in a planned residential community, you may have to seek approval from your homeowner association, which keeps watch on all residents and restricts activity that may hurt resale value or be a nuisance to neighbors. If you rent, be especially diligent and upfront with your landlord when starting a home-based business. Not doing so can get you evicted. If you are confused or facing issues with a business you are already operating, you can always contact a small business attorney, who can guide you through the gauntlet.

Second, check into getting a business license, especially if you are selling taxable goods or services online or from your home. The government requires business owners to get a business license so that revenue can be tracked for taxation purposes.

Third, find out if you need a general business license. This is a permit that lets you legally operate a business in your area. You may also be required to get a home occupation permit. This permit basically says that you are allowed to operate your type of business in your neighborhood.

Finally, there is the sales tax permit. This permit is required for you to collect state and local sales tax from your customers. At first, you may think you don't need this type of permit, and you may be correct, but check and recheck. If you don't have it and your state revenue agency catches wind of that fact, you could be in big trouble. Check out the SBA'a online article, "Sales Tax 101 for Small Business Owners and Online Retailers."

Business license and permit regulations vary from location to location. You may not need to worry about any licenses or permits, but check to make sure. The Small Business Administration (sba.gov) has a tool called "Permit Me" that helps business owners navigate the process. When you get on the SBA website, simply click on the "Permit Me" link and enter your zip code and the type of business you want to start. The site will then link you to information and applications to get started.

Separating Your Home Life from Your Work Life

Some people have started out with a business in their home, moved it to a separate location, and then moved it back to their home. After trying out both scenarios, they found that it was more economical and convenient to have their business located where they reside. Unless one is expecting a lot of foot traffic or needs to be in a business location, home base is the best place to be.

After talking to home-based quilting business owners, I've compiled some tips on making a home-based business workable.

Beyond Design

"At first, I had children at home; now I just love the convenience of working at home and having everything here," Therese May of Therese May Quilts (theresemay.com) says. "I've had several studios located in downtown areas of the city and enjoyed that, but I always found I still needed to work at home as well. Working at home is convenient and much more relaxing."

First, set boundaries and be diligent about keeping them. If you have small children, be clear in letting them know when they can disturb you and when they need to be quiet and play away from your workspace. Also, let them know which areas, equipment, and paperwork are off limits and that they shouldn't be constantly interrupting you. This is not to be mean to your children, but they could get hurt around your machines and tools, and you can get a lot more work done if you are undisturbed and allowed to work without interruptions. You might explain this to your children and also plan some uninterrupted time with them like you do with your work.

Second, decide on the hours you want to work and stick to that schedule. With that said, you must also realize there will be times when you are on a deadline and need to get an order out or a quilt finished. For the most part, though, if this is going to be a 10:00 a.m. to 4:00 p.m., Monday through Thursday business, try to stick to those hours. The fastest and easiest way to get burned out is to work all the time and never allow yourself any downtime. Home-based business owners will tell you that it can become all consuming. But when you set your business hours, stick to them. If the phone rings at 4:05 p.m., resist the temptation to answer it. Your business is closed.

A third tip is to be able to say no to family and friends, a difficult but necessary skill if you want your business to succeed. When friends find out you have a business in your home, some may not believe you are really working. They may show up to visit unexpectedly, call you, or want you to go to lunch whenever it is convenient for them. Family members may call and want you to do errands because, after all, you don't really "have a job." Don't fall into the trap of agreeing, and don't feel guilty about saying no. Explain to them that you are working and that maybe you can get together on your day off, or perhaps you will be able to help out some other time.

Finally, when you go into your work area, you need to be disciplined and work. This isn't the time to play around, call friends, or do personal projects. If you were at a job on someone else's dime, you wouldn't do those things. Don't do them now. This is your dime, so don't cheat yourself.

Finding Your Business Space

Let's face it: Everybody needs their space, and your business needs its own. Look around your home and find a place you can call your own, a place where you can have plenty of room, away from foot traffic so that it will be quiet and you can focus on work. It might be a place in your home such as a study, a transformed guest room, or basement, or a building at the back of your property or your garage. Designate this specific area of your house for your business workspace and office. The Internal Revenue Service wants business and only business to be conducted in your "business area," especially if you are going to claim a percentage of your home business space as a deduction on your taxes.

Remember, you will have a worktable, your sewing machine, your quilting machine (if you have one), file cabinets, and maybe your home office space. A closet, the kitchen table, or the middle of the living room won't work anymore. You will have too much to do to worry about picking up at the end of every day, and you will no doubt need more room to spread out. You may have several projects going at once, or you may need to make calls. Either way, your surroundings need to be quieter than the living room, especially if you have small children.

After you choose a workspace, you'll need to think about your home office. This is the place where you will contact customers or clients, get your orders ready to go, and do a host of business-related activities. Because you already have a room dedicated to your business, you could locate your home office in a corner of this room. It would be convenient to have your office here, as you will no doubt be going to your computer many times a day to answer e-mail, take customer orders, and more. You need a place big enough to put a desk that can hold your electronic equipment and space to write down orders and notes on those orders.

Setting Up Your Space

While you won't need much in the way of office furniture, there are a few things every office needs. Having everything related to your business available will make bookkeeping much easier. Some things you may already have. Some things may be readily available and you just have to purchase them and put them in your business area. Read through this section to get started on your office.

Furniture

The first thing you need to think about is a desk. It doesn't have to be big or fancy, just something to get the job done. You can start off with a card table or make your own by using two two-drawer file cabinets for the leg portion and laying a board on top of them at whatever length you want your desk to be. You might also consider checking secondhand stores. Sometimes they have desks that are cheaper than card tables. Also, get the word out to your friends who work for businesses. One hospital in my area is always giving away desks, file cabinets, office chairs to people who can haul them away. I know of a local oil company that gets rid of office furniture as well. Spread the word among your friends who work at businesses like these and tell them that if their company is disposing of items, you might be in the market.

Second, find a good office chair. At first, a metal folding chair will work fine, but if you find yourself sitting for long stretches in front of the computer, you may want to go out and invest in a chair sooner than you expected. Go to several stores and sit in a lot of chairs to see how they feel. Make sure your feet can touch the floor and that you have good lumbar support. Because everybody's body is different, chairs will fit people in many different ways. While the cheapest chair doesn't usually offer great comfort, I have found the highest-priced isn't always the best, either.

You will also need a file cabinet at some point. You can start with two drawers and then later expand to four. In your file cabinet, you can keep things like orders and paid invoices. You can also keep hard copies of patterns, receipts for taxes, and any other paperwork related to your business. You may think everything will store much easier on your computer. While that will save you floor space, lose one record and you'll wish you had gone old school and kept *some* things in a file cabinet.

Phone

Today, many businesses are operated with a cell phone. That's a good choice if you get good reception. However, if you live in an area where you are constantly getting dropped calls, have poor reception, or experience constant static, invest in a landline. This is an essential tool for helping you stay in touch with your customers and clients. If you already have a landline, you might consider another line if you have teenagers in the house.

If you do get a landline just for your business, have it located where your business is. This should be a quiet location, which is exactly what you want when you are conducting business. You want a quiet area where you can talk and where your client can hear what you are saying.

If you can't afford to get a separate landline, invest in a phone system that will alert the rest of the household when you are on the phone. There are systems that flash or will show "line in use." It is very unprofessional when you are in the middle of a conversation to have someone else pick up the phone somewhere else in the house. Even though you have a home business, people expect you to run your business as if it wasn't.

For occasional faxes, check out MyFax.com. This company allows you to send and receive faxes from your computer over the Internet. MyFax will be cheaper and more convenient for you than a landline fax. You won't have to buy a fax machine and you don't have to get a dedicated fax line. Another big plus about using this company is you can see what faxes you have received by simply checking your email wherever you are.

The Indispensable Office Engine: Your Computer

At one time, you could have gotten away with not owning a computer and running a business. That is not the case anymore. Computers are an essential and necessary part of business these days. They store all types of data and help you recover that data quickly and easily. Because you will probably be doing everything yourself—communicating with clients, filling orders, doing bookkeeping, designing patterns—your computer will be your workhorse.

A computer will also help you market your business. You will find that it is your biggest asset when it comes to marketing. Let's say you want to run an ad in the paper. In the past, you would have had to draw out your ad, take it down to the local paper, have them make a mock-up of it, and you'd have to either wait around for it or come back later to approve it. If you wanted changes, you'd have to make additional trips to the paper, taking even more time. Now all you have to do is contact the paper via phone or email, tell the professionals what you want and then it can go back and forth via email in the form of attachments. The paper will send it back to you once they get the proofs, which is the final copy, ready for your approval. Once you give the go-ahead, they will drop it in the paper. You can then pay the newspaper or magazine for the ad via check or electronic payment.

Of course, there are still a lot of people who are resistant to owning and operating a business with a computer. I get it. A computer can be intimidating. There is a learning curve when it comes to learning how to operate one. If turning on a computer and pushing buttons terrify you, take a computer class at your local vocational school or grab a teenager to show you. The younger generation has no qualms when operating anything electronic. They jump in and never look back. In no time and with a little practice on your part, you will be operating your computer like a pro and you'll wonder why you were so hesitant in the first place. Consider these areas where a computer can help you in building your business.

Advertising

A computer gives a home-based business owner so many options when it comes to advertising. You can build a website and have your storefront open seven days a week, twenty-four hours a day, every day of the year. A website is an easy way to get people familiar with your business, what you do, how much you charge, your professional skill and expertise, and how to contact you. If you teach or speak on certain areas of your business, clients will want to know about it. And they should be able to read about it on your website.

If you want to print flyers, brochures, invoices with your logo, or business cards, it's easy to do with a computer. You can find sites on the Internet that have templates you can download to easily design all of these and more. Once you have downloaded the templates you want, all you have to do is fill in the blanks. We'll discuss more about promotional material, including websites, for your business in a later chapter.

Bookkeeping and Tax Records

Many people groan when bookkeeping and taxes are mentioned, but your computer can help make these issues much less painful. With your computer, you can build spreadsheets using Microsoft Excel or iWork Numbers on a Mac. This will allow you to separate and chart expenses such as gas, postage, reuseable items such as fabric and fusing, and tools and equipment you purchased through the year. You will also be able to input how much you are being paid for each job you do. After you subtract your expenses from your revenue, you will see how much you are making at any given time.

For instance, let's say you teach a class across town. You prepare for fifteen students and you make sixty dollars per student. That's nine hundred dollars. Now it cost you three hundred dollars for supplies and one hundred dollars for gas and food, so after subtracting that amount, you will have a profit of five hundred dollars, from which you will then need to take out taxes.

It is important to keep records and receipts for all you do. If you are using a computer and spreadsheet, you can add all your expenses in categories at the end of the year. You will know how much you spent for fabric, photocopies, and other items. You should also make a spreadsheet to track those who have paid you for jobs and any money outstanding. All this will make doing your taxes easier, as you will have all the information you need, organized in the way you need it.

Building a Database

You will need to start building a database as soon as you start your business. A database containing contact information on your clients, contacts, and vendors will make a big difference in how efficient your communications are with them. Once you have built your database, you can send out postcards or e-mails when you have a new product, a special sale, or just want to remind your clients of what you do. Maybe you are going to be at a trade show or quilt event in Savannah, Georgia. You have a number of clients there and you want them to come and see you at the event. You would simply go into your database, search for your clients in and around Savannah, and zap them an e-mail about when, where, and how long you will be there. If you are teaching a class, send out announcements to all those students who have taken your classes before. If they can't come, they might know someone who wants to and can.

By keeping vendors or suppliers in your database, you can contact them easily if you need a large amount of something quickly. Maybe you have just contracted a huge quilt job. You are going to need many yards of fusible material, and with your database up to date, you can go in, pull the suppliers you know have large amounts of fusing, and send them all an e-mail at the same time requesting pricing, ship dates, etc. Contacting several people at once makes more sense than calling them one at a time.

Communication

One of the best ways a computer can assist you is by allowing you to communicate with your customers through the Internet and e-mail any time of the day or night. If there are quick questions that need to be answered, follow-up discussions that need to take place, or a question or problem you need to discuss with a vendor and it's midnight, e-mail is always available to you. This form of communication can save you time and headaches. There are times when a phone call is appropriate, but use the Internet to your advantage. Besides all the other advantages, you will have a paper trail; if you need to go back and see what was said, you will have it in black and white.

Designing

A computer can also help you when you are designing quilts. You may not have immediately thought about designing quilts on the computer, but with today's new technology and the programs available, if you have a creative streak, you might want to try it. Designing on a computer will not only allow you to see your finished product, but if you want to sell your patterns and designs, a computer can help you store those designs, ship them out, and receive payment for them.

Keeping Inventory

As you start your business, you will need to keep a running inventory. Your inventory will let you see what you have and what you need at a glance. Also, when tax season comes around, you will know what you've sold through the year and what you still have on your shelves. A tax accountant can help you set up your particular records so you will know how to input specific information. Remember too, if you get it set up right the first time, you won't have to worry about it later.

You may have a set price for a specific type of quilt you make and sell. Perhaps you have patterns or quilting kits you market and sell through your business. A computer can help you keep track of all those items you sell. You can categorize your items in a spreadsheet, make changes in a snap when you need to, and update certain items when old ones go out and new ones come in or prices go up.

To The Point: Taming the Paper Tiger

After running a business for a while, you will find you have amassed a large number of receipts. In conjunction with your computer, a machine called Neat will help you keep all those receipts from overwhelming you. With the Neat (neat.com) scanner, you simply scan all the receipts into folders you have made on your computer. Fabric receipts can go in one file, gas in another, postage in another. At the end of the year, you can file these together, and if the IRS ever comes looking for your deductions, you can print them out or send the electronic file. There are two sizes of machines: a portable version for $150 and a desktop version for $400.

What Type of Computer Is Best for You?

Now that we've looked at what a computer can do for you, let's take a look at some specific computers and why they might work for you—and why they might not. For all the newest and latest innovations in the computer world, there are basically still two computer systems. One is the Microsoft Windows–based personal computers. The other is the Macintosh from Apple. Both will do what you need them to do for your business: bookkeeping, record keeping, keeping in touch with your clients and customers, and, should you be thinking of using a lot of graphics in your business, even graphic design.

With that said, before you go out and buy a Mac or a PC, make sure it will do what you want it to do. If you already own quilting computer programs or plan on purchasing some, check their requirement to make sure they'll work on the system you want and that your new computer is powerful enough to accommodate them.

Make a list of everything you want or need your computer to do. When you go computer shopping, take your list and ask questions. Buying a computer is a major purchase. You want to get one that's going to be an asset.

After you've decided on which system you'd like to use, you will need to think about whether a desktop, laptop, or notebook would work best for you. While notebooks may be the best thing when you travel, a notebook is too small for extended use, especially when you are doing books, designing, or writing a lot of e-mails.

This leaves desktops and laptops. If you are working in a confined space, a laptop may fit the bill. I know of many quilters who use laptops with seventeen-inch screens as their main computers. The laptop sits on a table when they are in their office and folds up to travel with them when they are on the go. While a laptop is convenient, it does have its drawbacks, mainly in the size of the screen. With that said, all laptops have the capability to allow the user to plug in a larger screen, so don't let the size of the screen stop you from getting one. On some laptops, however, you are limited as to how many add-ons you can plug in and how much expansion they can tolerate, so always ask about everything the laptop can do.

Desktops have and always will be the workhorses of businesses large and small. They aren't necessarily any better than laptops, but they do have the capacity to expand and do more things for you. Typically, they have six to eight USB ports, whereas a laptop may only be able to support four. You can add extra monitors instead of using just one. If you are planning on putting together quilting programs or perhaps burning your designs to disk, you'll want a desktop for its capabilities.

Of course, the ideal situation would be to have a desktop, laptop, and notebook, but that's not always realistic. If you already own a computer but haven't been using it for business, it would no doubt be ready for business in a few days with just a few tweaks.

If you don't own a computer, start saving your money and looking around. There are deals to be had on all models, shapes, and types. Computers can range in price from four hundred to five thousand dollars, depending on what type you get and what comes loaded on them. At certain times of the year, you can find great sales, especially in the fall when the manufacturers are getting ready to introduce their latest and greatest. Once again, don't be afraid to ask questions.

If you decide to go with a desktop, you will need to consider what size of monitor to get. Your decision should be based on your eyesight and the size of your office. Monitors can range in price from seventy-five to four hundred dollars. You might want to consider the new touch screen monitors as well. These will probably cost you more, but they may well be worth the price if they speed up your work.

Software and Accessories

Most computers will come loaded with some software. You might want to play around with what you have, and if it doesn't work for you, you can always upgrade.

You will most certainly need a good accounting program. I like Quickbooks or Quicken. These programs are dedicated to bookkeeping and have features that will make your life easier not only throughout the year, but when tax time arrives. Another program you will need is a general software package that includes a word processing program, spreadsheet and database, e-mail organizer, calendar, and to-do list. You'll also need to look for a program that easily converts documents to PDF. In the past this wasn't as much of an issue, but these days more and more people want documents in PDF form. Microsoft Office covers all those bases. The program isn't cheap, but once you purchase it, Microsoft offers updates and upgrades for little or no cost to you.

Once you get your business software, you will probably want to look for business-specific software, like quilting programs to help you design quilts or enhance the designs you already have. Like everything else, programs come and go. You should do research—not only on the Internet, but also when you attend shows and festivals—to find the best programs for the type of quilting and work you do.

Of course, you will need to consider getting a printer, scanner, copier, and fax. You can buy all of these separate, or you can get an all-in-one machine. All-in-ones have all four capabilities and will be cheaper than buying four separate machines. They will take up less space and will no doubt be easier to set up. Most of these machines use wireless technology these days, thus eliminating the need for cords spanning the length of a room. All-in-ones can range in price from $150 to $500. The only real disadvantage to owning an all-in-one is that if one part of the machine breaks down, you lose all four machines while it is being repaired.

Internet Connections and Power Supply Protection

When you get your computer equipment set up, you will need to decide how you want to communicate with the rest of the world on your computer—via cable modem, DSL (digital subscriber line), or satellite. While any of these modes will work, go with broadband or satellite if financially possible. These tend to be more reliable and run faster. Of course, go with what is available to you and what you can afford. Sometimes you may not have any choice, but if you do, try to stay away from dial-up. Dial-up has for the most part gone the way of the dinosaur, and for good reason. It is so slow that children were going from diapers to graduation hats before they could complete their first search.

Next, consider getting some type of backup power for your computer. If you have a laptop, a battery will already be included, but if you find the battery power included is insufficient, ask about batteries with nine-hour life spans. They are available.

Two other items you might think about are a surge protector and a UPS (uninterrupted power supply). A surge protector will keep your equipment from getting zapped if you have unstable electrical lines or if you live in an area where there are a lot of electrical storms. Even though you may unplug your equipment if a storm is headed your way, what if you are away from home and you don't know when an electrical spike is traveling down the line into your home? If your computer has ever gotten fried, you will appreciate the money you spent to keep that from happening again.

Then there are UPS devices. Imagine you're on your computer working away and the power goes out. If you don't have a battery backup that allows you time to save your work, you can lose everything you have been working on. With a UPS, you typically have fifteen to thirty minutes to finish up your work and get off the computer before everything goes black.

Most UPS devices will have a built-in surge protector. They range in price from $75 to $250, but they are well worth the expense. Consider it a little piece of insurance and peace of mind.

Small Office Supplies

Once your big purchases are made, you will need to consider some small office supplies: clock, calculator, calendar, paper, envelopes, tape, scissors, stapler with staples, paper clips, letter opener, file folders, pre-inked stamps, postage scale, and pens and pencils. These items may seem trivial until you need them. You can purchase them when you find them on sale and when you have the money.

A wall clock is a good choice, as there won't be anything to obstruct your view and you can glance up at the time easily. A desk calculator is a better choice than a small pocket calculator or the calculator on your computer. While these are great in a pinch, having printed tape will be a lifesaver when you start doing complex calculations.

Patchwork

Keep a list of small items like calendars, calculators, pens, pencils, and quilting pins. When holidays or your birthday roll around, ask your family and friends to buy you these items.

Dollar stores are a great place to find some of these items at a great price. Also, stores have these items on sale when they put out school supplies or they are getting ready to inventory at the end of the year. I can often find a one-hundred-count box of plastic coated paper clips for a dollar. Look around in your area and you will probably find comparable sales.

Business Bank Account

If you haven't done so yet, now is the time to open your business banking account. This will need to be a separate account from your personal one. When tax season rolls around and in the long run, having a separate account makes sense. Call your bank to see what you need to bring to set up your account. The kind of documentation you will need will depend on how you have set up your business: sole proprietorship, corporation, LLC, or partnership.

If possible, set up your business account with the bank where you have your personal account. In today's electronic age, you can transfer money electronically from your business account to your personal account, thus saving you money on check fees. Also, if you are dealing with a bank you have done business with in the past, you shouldn't have trouble putting checks in and being able to use your money immediately. With new accounts at new banks they sometimes want to hold your money for seven to ten days. Be forewarned that if you deposit a large check, sometimes even over five hundred dollars, your bank will hold it until it clears, anyway. Just account for that when you are planning your budget and you will be fine.

You might want to open a savings account at the same time you open your business checking. You will have expenses throughout the year, and having some money put away in savings will help you manage when expenses come due. Two of the biggest cuts will be Uncle Sam and insurance. You should plan to put 33.3 percent back for the Internal Revenue Service and at least 10 percent for insurance. (Some economists recommend 20 percent.) By making savings a priority, you will be ahead in the long run. If you have money left over at the end of your fiscal year, you can invest in new equipment or stock up on inventory.

Insurance Needs

If you own or operate your own business, be it at home or elsewhere, you need to think about insurance. Granted, a home-based business may not need a lot of coverage, and each business varies depending on its size and where it conducts its business. However, there are certain types of insurance you will want to get and others you should consider.

First, you will want to find a reputable company and a dependable agent who can help you set up your insurance. Your insurance company needs to have been around for a while. You don't want to get involved with a company that's going to close its doors after a few years in business, leaving you with paid premiums but no coverage. Your agent should know his business and be straightforward, helping you get the coverage you need without overselling. You shouldn't be afraid to ask your agent questions, and if he won't or can't answer your questions to your satisfaction, look for another one. If you don't have an agent or are in the market for a new one, you can always contact the Independent Insurance Agents and Brokers of America. You can visit their website at iiaba.net or call (703) 683-4422.

Be aware of your state's requirements and restrictions regarding insurance. Most states have websites that list their statutes and rules related to insurance codes. If you are working by yourself, do your work from your home, and have no customers or clients who come there, you're not going to need much insurance. There are a few types you do need to consider, however.

Home Business Insurance

If you own a business in your home, talk to your agent about a home business insurance policy. This type of insurance covers your business property located in your home—e.g., your sewing machine, computer, and other business equipment.

Don't assume your homeowner's policy will cover these business items, as most don't. Some insurance companies do offer special riders on their policies that can include business property, but you have to ask for it. These can be quite expensive.

A straight home business policy can be less expensive, but there are exclusions, so be sure to investigate thoroughly before paying your premiums. If you have a separate building out back for your business, tell your agent and make sure your insurance will pay for fire, storm, water damage, and any burglaries.

Health Insurance

You may already be covered if your spouse works. However, because health insurance is a part of the American landscape, if you don't have it, you will need to look into getting it. There are different levels of health insurance available. If you are not covered under a spouse's insurance and you are self-employed, you may find yourself having to pay a healthy premium, especially if you find yourself sick a lot. If you are the healthy sort, you may be able to get by with a catastrophic plan. These typically have a high deductible and won't pay out for regular doctor's visits, but if you get seriously ill, it could save you a lot of money. Check out state-run plans and the Affordable Care Act options. They typically have better rates for self-employed people.

If you decide to hire employees, you will need to go back to your agent and talk to him about insurance for them. At that point, you may be able to create a group policy, depending on the number of employees you have and what you are willing to spend for group insurance.

There may be other types of insurance you need or are required to have in your particular state, city, or county if you have a home-based business. Be sure to ask your agent if he knows of any. If he doesn't, you might want to consider checking with your state insurance commissioner. You don't want to be fined or have your business closed down for something you didn't know you were supposed to have.

Your First Commissioned Works

Perhaps you've made quilts on your own for a number of years. Now someone has approached you about making a quilt or finishing one for them. While you may already have a reputation for quality work, let's discuss some work habits you must develop if you want your business to be a success. These aren't difficult, and chances are you already incorporate them into what you do. If so, great—consider this a review. If you haven't been doing these things, start with your next job. It is vital for your success. Here is an overview of what you should be doing:

Always get a bid/estimate approved and signed by your new client. You might not think this is a big deal, but if you spend time making or finishing a quilt and your client comes back and says it's too much to pay, you'll think it's a big deal. Getting an estimate or bid approved and signed by the client is like a contract. It protects you and your customer.

You will want to be as detailed as possible in your bid. Put down the pattern your client wants, what the material to make the quilt will cost, and estimate how many hours it will take you to make or finish it. Then total the amount and see if the client is okay with the price. If so, get a signature. Keep a copy and give him or her a copy. With a signature on paper, your client can't come back and cancel because of the expense.

Discuss both your and your client's expectations. Talk to your client about what is most important with the project. Let your client know when you can have the quilt ready and ask if this is okay. If the quilt is to be a wedding gift and the wedding is two days away, it might be unrealistic to expect you to finish the quilt in time. But if the wedding isn't for a month and that's doable for you, then definitely let the client know and have the project done when you promised it would be.

Make sure the details are correct. If color is a big deal for your client, write down what your client wants and stick to it. A good rule is to show your client fabric swatches so you can get the color just right. Also ask your client what colors you should avoid. Don't put in a section of pink pattern if pink is on the "Don't like" list. If the client chooses a color from your swatch and you can't find that exact color, get as close as you can and then get the client's approval before you start the project. It would be a shame to make an entire quilt only to find your client doesn't want it because the color is wrong.

Be professional. There are always disagreements that could arise between you and your client, but don't get caught up in an argument. As they say in retail, the client is always right. Try to remedy the situation as best you can, but if it can't be remedied, bow out gracefully.

When meeting a client or attending a fair or festival, dress appropriately. You don't have to dress in a suit, but don't come in jeans with holes in them or short shorts. You want people to see you as a responsible business owner, someone they can trust when they come to you to make something for them. Likewise, don't drink alcohol when meeting a prospective client. You want to be sharp and on your game. Smoking isn't a good idea either. These days there are many people who can't abide the smell of cigarettes. If you smoke, clients may be afraid their quilts will come to them smelling like cigarettes. That may be enough for them to look for another quilt maker.

Invoice your client. When the work is done, write an invoice before you hand over the product to your client. Put the client's contact information on the invoice and make a few notes on your copy. You never know when you will make a quilt and need to figure out which clients might be interested in it. Always give your client a copy of the invoice with your contact info on it. That way he'll have your info if he ever wants you to make another quilt. Give each invoice a unique name or number. You can use the client's phone number or his last name. By doing this you can file your invoices and be able to find them easily.

You may want to consider getting a down payment for the work before you start. When you first begin, you may not be able to do this. Clients may be hesitant to pay someone they don't know yet. After all, how can they be sure you won't take their money and skip town? However, on the flip side, also imagine that you dog all the work and then your client never comes to get the quilt.

Pay yourself. After you get paid for the project and put the money in the bank, it is time to pay yourself for all your hard work. There are expenses you will need to deduct from the total amount before you get your money. Remember, you will need to take off the materials you used for the project and a percentage for taxes and insurance before you take your part.

Let's take a look at this with numbers. You gave your client a bid of $650 for a queen-size quilt. You spent $104 for fabric, $56 for batting, and $24 for thread. That totals $184. You need to take out $216 for taxes and $65 for insurance and put it away in savings. When all that is subtracted, you will have $185 left over to take free and clear. At first that may not sound like a lot, and if it feels like you are working for free, consider raising your prices. If it takes you twenty hours to make a quilt and you have to make at least $25 an hour to make ends meet, make sure to figure that into the estimate or bid at the beginning. Be careful not to price yourself out of the market. At the beginning, you may have to take less than you feel you are worth, but once your clients find out about you and the quality of your work, you will be able to ask for more.

So you can get a better idea of how project costs break down, let's put it in chart form:

JOB: WEDDING RING QUILT

Bid Amount	$650
Paid on 04/16/13	$650
Material Costs:	
Fabric	$104
Batting	$56
Thread	$24
Taxes (33.3 percent)	$216
Insurance (10 percent)	$65
TOTAL	**$465**
Total Paid to You	**$185**

05 | Building a Team

You might think this is a rather odd chapter to have in a home-based business book, but I hope this chapter will give you something to think about if you ever want to expand your business. You will need internal team members in your business and, perhaps in the future, external team members. We will talk about both here.

Your internal team members will be the backbone of your business and your support personnel. They are people like bankers, accountants, and attorneys. You will pay just some of these team players, but all of them will be working with and for you. Choose carefully. These people can be the difference between having a strong business or one that will collapse under your feet.

Your external personnel will be your part-time helpers, employees, or any other personnel you choose to help you with your business. These people should be chosen just as carefully as your internal team, as they will represent your business and, in some cases, you will work in close proximity with them on a daily basis.

Now, let's take a look at both of these groups.

Your Internal Team

When looking for your internal team members, take your time until you find the right fit. Don't use your next-door neighbor's brother's accountant because he's convenient. Take the time to interview these people, as you will work closely with them. You want them to not only be affordable and capable, but to have integrity, be trustworthy, and have your best business interests at heart. By sitting down and talking to them, you can weed out the ones you wouldn't like to work with and find those who would be an asset to your business.

If you are already in business, think about the five following qualities when gathering your internal team.

1. *Accessibility*. Are you going to be able to talk to this person when you need to? If you can't get through to your attorney when you have a legal question, or your banker never calls you back when you need a loan for a new piece of equipment, what good are they? Sure, you won't need to call them every day, or maybe not even every year, but when you need them, you need to make sure you can reach them.

2. *Compatibility*. Does the professional know your line of work, and can he or she offer advice when you need it? Your internal team should be familiar with home-based businesses and know the challenges home-based business-people face. Can you speak freely to these people, and do you trust the advice they give you? Are they easy to talk to, and do they listen to what you are saying? You don't want anyone to patronize you.

3. *Ethics*. Can you trust this person? Does this person have integrity? Does he do what he says he's going to do when he says he'll do it? If she misrepresents herself, works in gray or shady ethical areas, or fudges here and there, she may do the same thing to you and your business. Ask around about the person you are thinking about working with. You will find out quickly what others think about her ethics and moral fortitude.

4. *Price*. While you will not have to pay a banker to work with you, you will have to pay your accountant and attorney. You don't have to get the most expensive ones, but you don't have to get the cheapest, either. After investigating the person's qualifications, experience, and skills, you should be able to find a decently priced professional who can help you with all your needs.

5. *Qualifications*. Make sure the professional you hire has the skills, background, and training to do what you need him or her to do. As mentioned before, find someone who is familiar with home-based businesses. You probably shouldn't hire someone who only does accounting part-time, and you might want to avoid someone who has just started out in the business. While there are advantages to hiring someone who is new, a seasoned professional may give you greater peace of mind, especially if you ever get audited or have to go to court for any reason. Check into these people's backgrounds. Where did they get their training? How long have they been in practice? How many clients do they have?

Think about these five areas as you look for your internal team. A few years down the road, you will be glad you did. Now let's take a quick look at the professionals who will help you build your business.

Your Banker

The first person you want to build a relationship with is a banker. If you have had your personal banking account with a specific bank for a while, go in and talk to the bank president. Typically, your personal bank will be more than willing to talk to you about a home-based business account, especially if your account has always been in good standing.

Your banker will be the first person you go to when you want to expand your business, need a business loan, or need a check processed quickly so you can make payroll or pay pressing bills. Your banker can work with you to set you up a line of credit and offer valuable financial advice.

As far as the bank you choose, that will be up to you. If you live in a small town, your only choice may be your small community bank. Sometimes, those banks are the best, anyway, because of the personal service they offer. You will want to choose a bank that is friendly and willing to help you with your business needs. If you live in a large city, you can still find small community banks, but you may want to go with a larger bank because it can offer more services like business credit cards, larger loans, direct deposit (or, these days, mobile deposits) and online banking. Be careful though. These extra services can also mean more service fees.

Your Accountant

How much business you do at first will determine whether you need to find an accountant right away or if you can wait a while. For most people, an accountant is someone they use once a year to get their taxes done, but an accountant can do much more than that for a home-based business.

An accountant can advise you on what business expenses you can legally make for a home-based business. If you want to expand or buy a new piece of equipment, he or she can also discuss which purchases would give you the best tax breaks. An accountant can also help with tax planning, profit and loss, audits, and monthly statements for paying your monthly state and federal taxes. When choosing an accountant, make sure he or she is qualified to do the work you want done, has a good reputation in the community, is familiar with home-based businesses, and has been doing taxes for a while. A certified public accountant (CPA) is the way to go if you can afford it. CPAs have met their state's educational requirements, have college degrees, and have passed a certification test and ongoing annual educational requirements. They are more expensive than a regular accountant, but they are up on all the new tax laws and any changes. The extra money you pay will be worth it in the long run, especially if you ever run into tax problems.

Your Insurance Agent

If possible, find an agent who can handle all your insurance needs. At first, all you may need is a home-based business plan that protects your business equipment and health insurance. Most agents work for one agency but have access to several different insurance companies, so this shouldn't be a problem.

You might want to start with the agent who carries your vehicle or homeowners insurance. If your own agent can't help you, he or she probably knows an agent who can. When looking for an agent, you want to choose one who doesn't undersell or oversell you insurance you don't need. You also want someone familiar with home-based businesses, good qualifications, and substantial experience in the services you need.

Your Attorney

You may think you'll never need an attorney, and maybe you won't, but even if you don't retain one on a regular basis, you should have one in mind in case you ever do need one. An attorney can assist you in writing up the correct legal structure for your business and file the papers for you. He or she can write a partnership agreement and represent you in court if, heaven forbid, you are ever sued or need to sue someone. Also, an attorney can also help you write a will and represent you in bankruptcy court if need be.

The attorney you're looking for will need to be skilled in business law and handle business matters. A criminal or civil attorney won't be able to help you here. Your attorney also needs to understand the needs of small businesses. The Small Business Administration may be able to point you in the right direction if you're not sure where to start.

Finding an attorney can be an intimidating process. But remember, you are building a business and need to watch out for your best interests. Having an attorney in mind is better than waiting until something happens and having to take the first one you find. By preparing in advance, you'll be able to handle any situation that may come your way.

Your Product Sales Representatives

Get to know the people you buy your supplies from. In your case, it will be your machine dealerships and your fabric and thread suppliers. Managers are the best people to talk to; that way, if you have a problem with regular staff, you can contact the manager and get things worked out.

Don't hesitate to meet with them, ask them questions, and talk to them about sale prices. You are one of the people who keep them in business and will continue to buy from them if they treat you fairly, so don't take any snubbing from them. They should take the time to talk to you and be happy about doing it.

As your business grows, you may need to get acquainted with other professionals, but for now these are the basic five. They can help you grow your business and direct you to other sources when needed. Even if you don't require assistance right away, keep their cards in your Rolodex. You never know when these will come in handy.

Your External Team

At first, your external team members may be just you. Perhaps it will always be just you, but if you ever want to expand or if you get snowed under with lots of work, you may need to think about hiring employees. You may not need many. Many home-based businesses only need one or two extra people, and sometimes they may be seasonal—say through Christmas or the spring, depending on what kind of products you produce.

If you choose to hire employees, you will need to choose them as carefully as you chose your internal team members. The right employees can alleviate a heavy workload. The wrong employees can make your load heavier and possibly put your business in danger of failing.

The Worker Pool

There are three types of people who can help you with your business: full-time employees, part-time employees, and subcontractors.

Full-time employees will pull eight-hour shifts five days a week and will come to your home office every day. If you decide to hire full-time employees, be sure to have enough work to keep them busy while they are there. Because you will be paying them, you want them doing something instead of just sitting around twiddling their thumbs. Full-time employees could be utilized to answer phones, take orders, fill orders, and get them ready to mail out. You just need to be sure your business is busy enough to keep a full-time employee occupied five days a week.

Remember when thinking about hiring full time employees that they will cost you money. Besides paying their salaries, you may need to train them. If they work over forty hours a week, you will have to pay overtime. Typically, you'll also have to pay workman's comp and federal and state taxes on the employee as well.

If you don't have enough work to hire a full-time employee, you might want to consider hiring a part-time employee. You may need someone to come in and work four hours a day, two days a week, or you may just need someone to come in and help in December when everyone is buying items for Christmas.

Your work may pick up during the summer, or you may want to go on vacation and need someone to watch over your business while you are gone, especially if you have a mail-order business and you send out supplies on a regular basis. While you still may have to train that person, once he or she knows your way of doing things, you can go on with your work knowing these tasks are being done well.

Patchwork

Make a list of jobs you need done on a daily, weekly, or yearly basis. After your list is complete, write a job description for each job on the list. Look carefully at this list and decide if a part-timer will work or if you need a full-time employee.

By hiring a part-time employee you will be able to gauge whether you need a full-time employee. If you need someone more than two days a week, go up to three, but always make sure the work is there.

A good pool to draw part-time employees from would be retirees and moms who like to work with quilts and whose kids are already in school. Some home-based quilting business owners have found it beneficial to barter work. A part-time employee may agree to work a few afternoons a week in exchange for quilting or sewing lessons. If this is an arrangement that benefits you, by all means do it. All parties involved will benefit from the arrangement.

Make sure you talk to your part-time employee and that he or she understands the arrangement up front before moving forward. You don't want any type of misunderstanding.

A third option is to work with an individual as a subcontractor. These can be additional workforce bodies without all the hassles of traditional employment. Subcontractors will do things that you need done but don't have the time or equipment to do yourself. They have their own business and are responsible for their own taxes, insurance, and other business expenses. An example of a subcontractor in your line of work would be a longarm quilt finisher.

Let's say you design quilts. You make the quilt tops, but you don't have the time or inclination to "finish" the quilts. You get a bid in writing from a person who has a longarm machine and whose business is quilt finishing. When you get the top ready, you send it to the quilt finisher. This person finishes it and you write out a check. The subcontractor's part of the job is now done. You now can sell your quilt for whatever price you want and not worry about anyone else taking a cut.

As with full-time or part-time employees, you will want to ask around and find out about a subcontractor's work ethics. You want to make sure anyone you hire is willing and ready to work for you, no matter what you ask or need them to do.

Where to Find Help

You've decided you have enough business to need help, but where do you look to find help? Below is a short list of possibilities. You may have other ideas, so go with the ones that make sense to you.

- **Ads:** All newspapers, have help wanted sections. You can place an ad for anywhere from twenty to three hundred dollars, depending on the size of your ad and the circulation of the publication. Don't worry about anything fancy. "Help Needed with Quilting Business; Call (314) 555-1212" is enough. After chatting with someone on the phone, you can set up a longer interview if you think the person might be a fit. You can also post an ad on Craigslist (craigslist.com) under the jobs category for your area.
- **Word of mouth:** This method of seeking workers won't cost you anything and can sometimes be the most effective. All you have to say is you are

looking for help and that anyone who knows of someone who needs work should call you. Fabric stores are a great place to get the word out because employees typically know people in the area. Don't feel obligated to hire someone who has been referred, however. A referral should still go through your screening process.

- **Friends and relatives:** Sometimes you don't need to look any further than your friend and acquaintance circle. A word of caution: Don't put someone to work just because he is your friend or relative. Treat him as you would any employee, and let him know that is how it will be from the start. He will respect you for it later.
- **Bulletin boards:** Make signs or flyers stating what kind of worker you are looking for and leave them on community bulletin boards. Laundromats, libraries, fabric stores, and sometimes your local post office will have boards where you can post signs and flyers. Ask the manager or supervisor before you put up your sign; otherwise it may be pulled down the minute you leave.

What You Need to Know about Employee Rights

Before you decide to hire employees, be aware that you must follow US Department of Labor rules and regulations regarding employees. There is a standard minimum wage you have to pay your employees, as well as a set number of hours they can work. If they work over forty hours, you will have to pay them overtime. If you hire a minor, there are certain rules that apply specifically to their age and the hours they can work.

Discrimination is another issue you will have to deal with. The Civil Rights Act of 1964 protects employees from being discriminated against because of their race, gender, color, religion, national origin, smoking habits, weight, sexual orientation, marital status, or physical handicaps (unless those handicaps prevent them from doing their job). Sexual harassment is not tolerated in the workplace, and when you hire employees they should know up front where you stand on the issue.

You need to understand workplace safety and heed the rules and regulations outlined by the Occupational Safety and Health Administration (OSHA). Visit the website at osha.gov to learn about its workplace regulations and how to report a workplace accident.

As an employer, you are allowed to test your employees for drugs or alcohol if you suspect there is a problem on the job. Typically, employers test for illicit drugs such as marijuana, cocaine, PCP, heroin, or other harmful substances. Before you hire an employee, you can also run background and credit checks. There are limitations as to what kind of information you can request, and you must inform the prospective employee that you will be running a check.

Because rules and regulations change regularly, you will want to have the latest information for your business. You can get that information by visiting the United States Department of Labor's website, dol.gov. The government won't care that you didn't know something, so make sure you keep up to date.

What Your Employees Need to Know

Now, just as there are things you need to know when hiring employees, there are things your employees need to know when they are being hired. Don't expect them to read your mind and guess at what you expect of them. Be clear about your expectations when you hire them.

It would be worthwhile to sit down and write out your expectations. You can give this list to your employees. It doesn't have to be a company manual per se, but if you are dead set about some things, you can write them down a paragraph at a time in one or two pages, outlining what you expect.

For instance, you could include that there is "zero tolerance" for absences. Of course, you can make allowances for certain things like flu or a death in the family, but not showing up because they'd rather be shopping than at work shouldn't be tolerated. You can also cover excused absences and your tardiness policy in this paragraph.

In another paragraph, you could write down your dress code if you choose to implement one. Maybe you don't mind your employee coming to work in jeans, but short shorts and piercings everywhere on your employee's body might be a little much for you.

Next, you might want to write a paragraph about substance abuse. There should always be "zero tolerance" where alcohol and any illicit drugs are concerned. Not only could the employee get hurt, but so could you, other employees if you have any, and your workspace. Make it clear from the beginning that if any employee shows up under the influence, he or she will be dismissed immediately. Of course, there are always exceptions for over-the-counter and prescribed medications. Sometimes, to control a cough, cough medicine must be taken. Think through this issue. Decide what you will tolerate and write it down.

You also need to discuss workplace safety and legal issues. These can be separate paragraphs in your employee manual. Your employees probably won't be running around with scissors, but if you have a teenager who works part time, you might want to mention it just in case. You also have to address sexual harassment policies just in case, heaven forbid, the issue arises. Ideally, your employees can and will get along in a professional and civilized manner. Just in case, though, you should write down your views.

Later on, you may think of something else to add to your list. There is nothing wrong with amending your employee manual. It's done all the time. Just be clear in your paragraphs about what you want and what will happen to employees if they don't follow your rules.

At first, it will probably be fairly simple, especially if you only have one or two employees. If you ever decide to expand or need to hire more employees, you might want to add a little something about your business, when and why you started, what your goals are, and your business statement.

Hiring and Firing

The time has come when you are ready to hire your first employee. You may have several applicants or you may have just one. Your choice may be a friend or a total stranger. Whatever the case may be, take your time when hiring an employee and don't hire someone because of friendship or because you feel compassion for an unemployed acquaintance. You are looking for an asset for your company, and frankly, even though your friend may want a full-time job, if she can't sew, is unorganized, has a negative attitude, or is unmotivated, she might not be a good fit for a business you are trying to grow.

Pay Scale

When hiring, the first thing you need to look at is what to pay. Of course, you may want to pay your employee fifteen dollars an hour when in fact you can only afford ten. While you do have to pay minimum wage, you don't have to pay at the top of the pay scale either. Decide what you can afford and tell your employee. If he can't work for that amount, he can go elsewhere.

Applications

Before you get to that step, though, you will want to have your prospective employee fill out an application. You can typically find standard work applications online or at your local office supply store. This should include the applicant's name, address, phone numbers, past work experience, education, and other information applicable to the job. Give the application to your prospective employee, and have him fill it out and return to you. You may also want to request a résumé at this time. You certainly don't have to, but it has become standard practice for businesses to collect this along with the application.

Now that you have your prospective employee's application, look it over and decide which questions you want to ask in the interview. Don't be afraid to ask about information that raised other questions in your mind as you read over the paperwork. You might also want to ask about the applicant's history, just to get to know him a little better. You should also ask why he wants to work for your company.

Interviews

If you have never met this person, schedule the interview in a public place, like a restaurant, library, or coffee shop. You shouldn't invite people into your home until you get to know them. If you have several people who have applied to be your employee and one happens to be your friend, don't feel bad if you find someone else who is more qualified and whom you feel you can work better with. This is not a friendship contest. You need to hire the best person for the job regardless of who it is. You are running a business. It's not personal.

Know too that you will not get along with everyone you meet and interview. You may be interviewing someone who makes you uncomfortable from the start. Again, hire someone you think you can work with.

Take your time when choosing someone. At the end of the interview, thank the person for coming and tell him or her that you'll be in touch. Think about the person's reactions and demeanor during the interview. Keep in mind that the person may have just been nervous and stumbled over words or answers.

Background Checks

Before you hire a person, it is well within your rights as an employer to do background checks. You can contact companies like Peoplesmart (peoplesmart.com) and Good Hire (goodhire.com) to run these checks for anywhere from $20 to $150, depending on what you want checked out. You need to make sure this person is not in trouble with the law and can be trusted before he comes into your home office. One small business owner was surprised to find that her well-mannered interviewee had a warrant out for her arrest for selling narcotics.

Training and Probationary Periods

Once you have hired someone, you will probably need to take some time to train that person. Don't expect a new employee to know how to do everything right away. Besides, if you want things done a certain way, you need to show the employee how to do it according to your preferences..

You might want to set a probationary period to see if the employee is going to work out. This period can last anywhere from six weeks to six months. This protects you. Tell the employee up front how long the probationary period is and what you will be looking for during that time. After this amount of time has passed, you should be able to tell if she can do what you want her to do, if your personalities mesh, and if you are able to trust her to do her work efficiently.

If things don't work out with an employee during the probationary period or after, you will have to let that person go. You should, of course, give your employee a warning before you dismiss him. Firing someone can be unpleasant business, but it happens. There are some instances, though, that warrant an immediate dismissal, such as drug use and stealing from you.

When you do have to let an employee go, make sure to do it in a private location, not in front of other people. Be clear about why you are firing the person. Give the person his last paycheck and be civil. If you need to let your employees go because work has slowed down, talk to them before the fact, so they can start looking for other jobs. Even though they might not like looking for another position, they will appreciate the thoughtfulness.

Having and working with employees is never easy. Books like *Employment Law: A Guide to Hiring, Managing and Firing for Employers and Employees* by Lori B. Rassas and *The Hiring and Firing Question and Answer Book* by Paul Falcone go into more depth about hiring and firing employees. We only touched on the bare basics here. If you ever need to hire someone, think about the information in the second half of this chapter and consult the books listed above. It could save you a lot of headaches down the road.

Beyond Design

"When I started out, it was just me," Betty Hairfield of Betsy's Quilts says. "I hired one part-time employee, and she helped me for over ten years. When she passed away, I hired another employee with more energy. We revamped and reorganized, and before long I had to hire another part-time employee. Now, I have two part-time employees whose time overlaps, so I have both of them here from 11:00 a.m. to 3:00 p.m. One is my right hand. She custom pieces customers' quilts and binds them if needed. She sees what needs to be done and does it. My second employee is artistic. She arranges fabric by colors and helps customers choose colors. I don't have to tell her what to do either. She is proud of her work and it shows."

06 Writing a Business Plan

You may be asking yourself, "Why do I need a business plan?" After all, you know other people who have home-based businesses, and they don't have a business plan. First of all, a business plan is just smart business practice. It can be a blueprint or a road map that can help your business grow. Second, if you ever want to get a loan from a bank, you'll need one.

You are a small home-based business, so your plan will not be as big as that of a multilevel corporation. However, you still need to put together a plan to determine where you are going and how you are going to get there. Yes, your business is small. But putting together a plan can help you learn more about the kind of business you have and help you see the obstacles that may keep you from reaching your goals.

Perhaps what scares most people about business plans is they think it is going to turn into a big nightmare report like the ones they had to write when they were in school. Nothing is farther from the truth, and in this chapter we're going to break down a business plan into steps. If you take your time and work on one area until it is completed and then move on to another, pretty soon the entire plan will be done.

To the Point

Business plans typically aren't completed in one afternoon, so you want to start right away. It could take three weeks or three months. You are not in a competition with anyone else, so however long it takes is how long it will take. Work on it at your own pace and be thorough.

Defining the Business Plan

What Is It?

A business plan, simply put, is a roadmap for a business that gives directions for where it wants to go by offering a set of business goals and how that business is going to get there. Think of it as an investment in your business. It is similar to you sitting down with pen and paper and writing down your life's goals. The only difference is you are doing it for your business, and the business plan may contain several more ingredients, which we will cover in this chapter.

What Can It Do for You?

While a business plan cannot guarantee you will get a loan from a bank or that an investor will come running to drop money in your business, there are other things it can do for you.

First, it can help you clarify your business goals. You may have many, and they may be all over the map. By putting those goals down on paper, you can look at your business objectively and see if those goals are feasible. You may find that what you thought would be a great idea for expansion simply isn't.

Second, you will see if you can afford your goals and get a sense of how long it will take to reach them. After investigating how long it will take, how much it will cost, and how long it will take you to recoup an investment, you may change your mind about the direction of your business.

Third, a business plan will point out your business's strengths and weaknesses. If you want to expand in the next six months into something like longarm quilting, but you don't have an avenue for advertising that fact, you will have to rethink your strategy.

Finally, your business plan will help you identify your competition and describe your customers. This is important because it will show you what your competition is doing and how you can work your business better. In describing your customers, you will see the segment of buyers who will be interested in your products and services.

Business Plan Components

At first glance a business plan can seem quite daunting because it has so many parts. But just as you would take the many pieces of a quilt and piece them together, you can do the same thing with a business plan. In the next part of this chapter, we will break down the many sections of a business plan. I have included a checklist below that lists all those components and the order in which they should be included in the business plan. Read through it, and then we'll jump right in to breaking down each section.

Business Plan Checklist

- ❏ Cover sheet
- ❏ Table of contents
- ❏ Statement of purpose or business summary
- ❏ Company description
- ❏ Services
- ❏ Marketing plan
- ❏ Operational plan
- ❏ Management plan
- ❏ Personal financial statement
- ❏ Start-up expenses and capital
- ❏ Financial plan
- ❏ Appendices

Use this list to mark off the sections you have completed. You don't have to do these in any order. You might want to think about doing what looks easiest to you first. Whichever way you decide to tackle the project, I suggest making a folder on your computer and a hard copy folder to save all your work. On your computer store the completed components of your business plan. In the file folder, you can store your notes, rough drafts, and compiled information. By keeping everything together in these two areas, you'll be able to find and access all your records. You will need to update your business plan periodically, so keeping everything organized will save you time and ultimately money.

So let's get started. We'll look at each one of these components one by one.

Cover Sheet

This should take you no time at all to put together. A cover sheet is like the title page of a book. It gives some very basic information about your business and your contact information. You can do this before or after you've put your business plan together.

To make the actual cover sheet, open a blank document and go about one third of the way down the page. Center and type in your business name. Double-space and type "Business Plan" underneath your business name. You should bold these two lines and make the font a few sizes larger than the rest of your information. Don't use a fancy font. Times New Roman is the standard for business documents.

Enter down to the bottom of the page and type in your name, flush left. Go to the next line and enter the name of your business again. Then type any contact information, such as address, city, state, zip, phone numbers, fax, e-mail, and website URL (if you have one already).

Table of Contents

When you finish putting your plan together, you will need to make a table of contents. Just like in a book, your contents page will list the parts of your plan and where to find them. Because you might be including all the parts listed on the Business Plan Checklist, you can list those as your chapters. Make a sheet with those sections listed. Once you get your business plan together, enter the page numbers for each chapter. If you have subheads, I suggest you enter these last because you may combine sections, leave some out, or even add a few.

Statement of Purpose or Business Summary

The summary is the first thing people will see in your business plan. You should keep it to two pages or less, very professional and to the point. This is basically a summary of facts about your business. Think of it as a five-minute interview during which you need to make an instant impression.

In this part of your business plan, you will tell the reader who the business owners are, where you are located, what your business does, who your customers are, and what the future looks like for your business. If you are applying for a loan, this is the place where you will state how much money you want, what you need it for, how it will help your business grow, and how you plan on repaying it.

You will want to write this section with confidence. Be upbeat. Don't act unsure about your business or use words like *hope, maybe, not sure,* or *perhaps.* Speak clearly and confidently about what you need and want. The way you speak about your business will let others know the level of commitment you have for it. If you are not committed, no one else is going to be. Would you be willing to loan money to a business owner who says, "I'm going to *try* to make this work," or "I'll *try* to repay you"? No.

You might want to think about writing this section last; this will give you time to think about what you want. When you have finished with the rest of your business plan, you will have a clearer vision of your business, anyway.

Here is an example of what your overview should look like:

Homespun Treasures, a home-based quilting business, specializes in not only small quilted items to sell, but also king- and queen-size quilts. It was established in 2004 and is located in Hometown, Colorado. Kate Neiman is the owner of the business. She has been making quilted items since 1999. Homespun Treasures wants to borrow $30,000 to purchase a longarm quilting machine and an embroidery sewing machine.

With the money requested, Homespun Treasures will buy a longarm quilting machine, thus allowing the business to complete quilting projects more quickly and efficiently. The longarm machine will cost around $25,000 after attachments are purchased. This machine will cut our quilting time by a quarter. Homespun Treasures will also be purchasing an embroidery machine, which will cost around $5,000. The business makes a lot of heirloom quilts for weddings and showers. The individual squares we make before piecing the quilt together are embroidered with the names of family, wedding dates, birthdates, etc. This machine will help Homespun Treasures increase its volume and therefore make more sales. Currently, there is a six-month wait-list for quilts.

Company Description

This section is also an overview of the inner workings of your business. You will include paragraphs on your management team, business operations, objectives, goals, philosophy, ownership, industry, and marketing. In later sections, you will expand on these topics, so don't worry about writing too much here. These are merely overview paragraphs.

You may not need to include certain sections. You are a home-based business, and your management team might be you. Don't worry about leaving out things not relevant to your business.

The first paragraph you want to write is what kind of business you are in and what you do. Give a brief history, where you are located, and the legal entity your business falls under—proprietorship, partnership, corporation, or LLC. You then need to add a sentence explaining why you chose this type of business.

Second, you need to come up with a mission statement for your business. You might also use this as your slogan if it's short enough. This statement, which should be no more than thirty words, should tell why your business exists and its guiding standards." It needs to be simple and to the point yet reflect your business's personality and values. Here's an example:

> "Homespun Treasures sews love into every project we complete so our customers can have an heirloom to pass down for generations."

Next, you are going to write about your goals and objectives. Goals are targets you have to reach, and objectives are what you work on while trying to reach those goals. So write down three to five goals and discuss how you are going to reach them.

The next paragraph will discuss your business philosophy. You will need to write about what is important to you about your business and about business in general. Do you like being your own boss? Have you always wanted to have your own business and, if so, why?

Marketing is a crucial part of the business proposal. Anyone who reads your business plan will want to know how you intend to market it. (See chapter 8 for a more in-depth discussion on marketing.) For now, just briefly state to whom you are trying to market and why. You should also write about why these people want your services.

In the next paragraph, you will write about your industry. Before you started your business, you probably looked around, saw others running their own quilting businesses, and thought, "I can do that." Discuss where your business is headed. Is the industry large, or are there only a few people who do what you do? Have you seen businesses like yours fail? If so, what will you do to prevent yours from failing?

In your final paragraph, you will cover your business's strengths. How is your company different from the competition? How is it the same? How is it better? What do you bring to the business that will help it succeed? How is your business ahead of the competition, and how will it stay ahead?

Services
While you may have already stated what you sell and what you do, in this part of the business plan, you are going to write specifically about your products and services

and attach a price to each. For each specific, write down what it is, a short description, and the price. Here's an example:

> *Small items: baby bibs, table runners, pillows, hot mitts, baby blankets, and pot holders. Prices on these items range from $7 to $35.*

Marketing Plan

This is a section you will want to spend some time on because anyone who reads it will too. They will want to see how you plan to make your business succeed. A marketing plan is essentially how you intend to sell your products and services and to whom are you going to sell them. You will need to be specific in this section and prove to the reader that you know the business. With that in mind, be forewarned that you are going to have to do a bit of research because you are going to need primary and secondary resources.

The information you gather personally is considered your primary source, such as how many similar businesses there are in the area. Secondary sources are ones you gather from publications, websites, organizations, and government agencies. You can also find resources in the library.

The marketing section of your business plan should contain at least five sections:

- Economics of your business
- Overview of your customers or clients
- Competition
- Marketing strategy
- Sales forecast

First, you need to look at the economics of your business. Describe your potential market. How many people are interested in buying quilts, and what is the current demand? Do you have a waiting list? What are the growth trends in the quilting market? What do you see as growth potential in quilting? Is there room for growth, or has the trend come to a standstill? What obstacles do you face in building your business, and how do you plan to overcome them?

Second, you will talk about your customers or clients. You will want to speak specifically to who they are: Male? Female? Old? Young? Married? Single? Parents? Grandparents? Where are your clients located? Are they all over the country or from a specific region or state? What is their income level? Are they lower, middle, or upper class? What kind of education do they have? Do they have jobs, or are they stay-at-home parents? Are they looking for quality or a bargain? Third, you need to cover your competition. Who is it? Make a list of at least five to ten online or brick-and-mortar quilting businesses that you may compete against. What do they do? What do they sell? How long have they been in business? What are their prices? The following chart may help you as you gather your data. You can also think of this part as describing the advantages and disadvantages of your particular business.

After you have done your research, answer these three questions for each of the businesses you analyzed:

1. How is my business similar?
2. How is my business different?
3. How is my business better?

Worksheet for Competitor Analysis

Questions	Your Business	Competitor	Competitor	Competitor
Age of business				
Products to sell				
Services offered				
Price range				
Quality				
Reputation				
Reliability				
Specialties				
Payment methods (credit cards, personal checks, cash, or all three)				
Customers				
Advertising methods				
Owner's personality				

Once you have finished this part of your marketing plan, you should have a good idea about the economics of your business, your customers, and your competition. Now you will want to think about your business and what makes it unique. Why would someone come to you for a quilt or quilted items instead of going to your competition? After giving it some thought, write a paragraph about your uniqueness. This will become your brand or niche.

Next, you will want to write down your marketing strategy. Anyone who is reading your business plan will want to know how you are marketing your business. How do you plan to let people know about your business and what you do? Word of mouth? A blog? Do you belong to your local chamber of commerce? Do you pass out business cards? Do you attend quilt shows and festivals? Have you had fliers made? Do you run ads in magazines or local newspapers? If your business is new, have you written a press release and sent it to your local newspaper? (If not, you should.) You will also want to write down how much you intend to spend on promoting your business. After their initial investment of business cards, website, invoices, etc., most people will set a monetary budget.

Now start a new paragraph and write about how you price your items or determine what you will charge for classes or commission work. You'll want to compare your prices to those of your competitors and write about any sales or discounts you offer throughout the year. Also include how you collect your money—all up front or part up front (the rest when the project is finished).

Finally, you will need to write a sales forecast. To do this you'll need to look at the best- and worst-case scenarios for your business's finances. You will be looking month by month at what you've sold in the past and what you think you might sell in the future.

For instance, let's say you sold three quilts at $500 each and finished eight more for your clients at $150 each. You taught a class that netted you $500, and you sold fifty quilt kits for $80 each. Your total intake for the month would be $7,200 ($1,500 + $1,200 + $500 + $4,000=$7,200). Expenses for the month ran $2,900, which you will need to subtract, giving you $4,300. After taxes and insurance are taken out, you are left with around $2,500 a month. This would be your *best*-case scenario.

Now let's look at your *worst*. You sold one quilt at $500, finished four quilts for clients at $150, didn't teach a class, and only sold twenty-five quilt kits at $80. Your total for the month would be $3,100. After taking out your expenses, which were $900, you would have $2,200 left over for taxes, insurance, and your salary. You would end up with around $1,400.

By keeping track of what you are doing each month, you will be able to see which months are slow and which ones nearly run you to death. You can quickly see how you are doing and if you can afford other expenditures. The following worksheet will help you as you work through this section.

After you get all your numbers on paper, you can sit down and write your forecast. You'll be able to see where you've been and where you are going. By keeping records monthly you can adjust your work schedule accordingly.

Sales Forecast Worksheet

	Total	January	February	March	April	May	June
1) Money in bank at start of month	$1,700						
2) Money from sold quilts	$1,500						
3) Money from finished quilts	$1,200						
4) Money from teaching	$500						
5) Money from quilting kits	$4,000						
6) Money made from patterns or books	-0-						
7) Total for month (Add 2–6)	$7,200						
8) Expenses	$2,900						
9) Salaries paid (if any)	-0-						
10) Total payouts (add 8 and 9)	$2,900						
11) Profit for month (subtract 10 and 7)	$4,300						
12) Bank total (add 1 and 11)	$6,000						

Operational Plan

In this section, you will be writing about how your business operates. If you are the only person who works in your business, you can write a paragraph about what you do on a regular basis and how you handle customer service. If you have an employee or two, you should write about what they do and why their role is important to your business.

Next, write a few paragraphs about where your business is located and why you chose a home-based business. Here you can also discuss any permits, licenses, and insurance coverage you have and if there are any rules or regulations you must abide by at the national, regional, or local level. You should cover each of these areas individually, writing about what they cost and how they benefit your business.

You will want to put in some information about your inventory and suppliers in this section as well. Write down what you have in the way of inventory and its average value. Explain why you have inventory on hand and how it helps your business.

In the next paragraph, write about who your suppliers are. Make a list and include their names, addresses, how long you have been doing business with them, what you buy from them, how often you buy from them, and the average amount you spend when you do buy. Also mention if prices are higher than the norm, if you are given a discount, if prices have risen or held steady over the past year, and how your business has dealt with any rising prices.

In the last paragraph of this section, you will need to write about your credit policies, if you have any. If you require payment immediately upon delivery of product (cash and carry) and don't need to extend credit, you can explain that in this paragraph.

Beyond Design

Joan Knight of Quilts and Things says, "You have to make sure you are disciplined and organized, so as not to waste time and be unproductive. Keep good schedules and notes on teaching classes. Treat it like a job and be sure to make time for family by keeping regular work hours."

Management Plan

This section can run one to two pages, depending on how many parts apply to your business. Here you will be explaining the day-to-day management of your business. If you divide this into paragraphs as you did in the other sections, you can make your way through it in two or three simple steps.

Begin by writing about you—what you do, what you bring to the business, and any skill set you may have. After this page you will want to include your résumé. This shows investors and bank managers that you have a track record in your line of business. You will also want to discuss your plan for the business in the event you die or become incapacitated.

If you are the only employee, you can stop there. If not, you will need to list your employees, starting with the one with the most seniority. Write down what they do, what they bring to the business, and how they enhance it. You will also want to include their résumés after yours.

Your last paragraph should include your support team: your accountant, banker, lawyer, insurance agent, mentors, or consultants. You will need to include their contact information—address, phone, website, e-mail address—and indicate how long they have been working with you and how they help your business.

Personal Financial Statement

Personal financial statements are the standard for all business transactions these days. These statements will list your personal assets (what you own personally, whether it's paid for or not, like your home, car, etc.) and your liabilities (what you owe). Do not include any of your business assets like your longarm machine or sewing machine. Those fall into a separate category. If you have an accountant, he should be able to print you off a statement easily. If not, you will need to work on coming up with a statement yourself. The Small Business Administration has a blank personal financial statement form on its website that you can print and fill out, or you can use the following one.

Assets	Dollar Amount	Liabilities	Dollar Amount
Cash on hand		Accounts payable	
Savings account		Amount owed to banks, credit cards, loans, etc.	
Retirement account (IRA or other)		Car loan balance	
Money you have coming in		Mortgage balance on real estate (total)	
Life insurance (cash surrender value only)		Life insurance yearly payment	
Stocks and bonds		Other installment accounts (total owed)	
Real estate		Unpaid taxes	
Vehicle(s) present value		Other liabilities	
Other personal property		Total liabilities	
Other assets		Net worth (take total assets from other side and put here.)	
Total assets		Total (subtract liability total from net worth)	
Salary		As endorser or cosigner	
Other income		Legal claims and judgments	

Start-up Expenses and Capital

Every business, new or established, will have expenses, whether it's buying pens and paper clips for a bank office or buying straight pins for a sewing business. It's the nature of business. In the beginning of your business, you may not have very many start-up costs, especially if you already own quilting supplies and machines that you can use. But if you decide you want or need new machines or want to expand, you will need to know how much you want to spend to decide how much you need to borrow or save.

You may not know in the beginning how much you are going to need, and it's not always a good idea to ask for an exact amount. The Service Corps of Retired Executives (SCORE), an arm of the SBA, recommends you pad your figures by at least 20 percent when you are figuring start-up costs and expenses. For instance, if you wanted to buy a longarm machine that costs $4,000, you would make your request for $4,800. This is simplified, of course, but I think it makes the point. You'll want to be as accurate as possible with your figures, but you never know what will happen between the time you turn in your request and when you actually get the money. It's better to request a little more up front than have to go back after the fact.

If you need other items, such as machine attachments, fabric, or office supplies, list them. Once you have completed your list, you will need to explain why you need these things. Will they improve your productivity, help you branch out, or help you fill a gap?

Financial Plan

In this section, you will need to write how you intend to make money in your business, how much you will need to get started, and how much capital you are going to need to stay in business. If you are just now starting up but already have machines and supplies, or if you are your only employee, you may not need much start-up capital.

SCORE has worksheets on its website for profit and loss statements, projected cash flow, balance sheets, and a break-even analysis. Even if you decide not to use any of their forms, you might want to look at them for reference.

First, you'll want to do a twelve-month profit and loss statement. This is where you plug in the numbers to determine what it will take for you to be successful. You will be looking at what your business takes in, or your gross profit minus all your expenses: rent (if you have any), telephone, insurance, supplies, taxes, accountant fees, advertising, machine maintenance, and any other expenses you can think of. Remember to include irregular expenses, too, like quarterly taxes, annual dues to organizations, and other annual business fees.

Subtracting the two amounts will give you your net profit. Don't worry about getting every number right. Remember, you are working on a projection, not actual figures. You may know what your expenses will be, but you may not know exactly what your business will bring in. Estimate and then explain why you think your business will bring in that amount. Do you have projects lined up? Is business currently on the upswing? Are more and more customers contacting you? Do you have a lot of traffic on your website?

You can work on your twelve-month profit and loss at the same time you work on your cash flow projection. Use the cash flow worksheet provided to figure out exactly where your business is and where it is going. Once you determine how much you currently have (or will have) coming in and how much is going out, you will know the cash amount needed to run your business.

Appendices

After you finish your research, you'll want to compile your notes and other supporting material in an appendix. You can include awards you have won, brochures and fliers, business cards, recommendation letters, résumés, articles written about your industry or your own business, a list of your machines with serial numbers, and anything else that might be pertinent.

Don't worry if you don't have everything listed above in your appendix. You may not have brochures, articles, or recommendation letters. Just include what you have. This will be an ongoing project, so you can add and take away as needed.

Storing Your Work

After you get your business plan put together, buy a three-ring binder, organize your work, and put it all in the notebook. You can buy pocket folders to keep items that will go in your appendix. While you will have your hard copy, you need to keep an electronic copy as well. This way your business plan will be easy to access, update, and send when needed.

Cash Flow Projection Worksheet

	Opening day of business	January	February	March	April	May	June	July
Cash on hand								
Collected receipts								
Other money coming in								
Total cash available								
Expenditures								
Purchases								
Supplies								
Advertising								
Machine maintenance and repair								
Taxes								
Loan payments								
Wages (if you have employees)								
Vehicle expenses								
Insurance								
Accounting expense (if you have an accountant)								
Legal expenses (if any)								
Subtotal								
Owner's pay								
Total expenditures								
Cash position at end of month (subtract total cash available from total expenditures)								

07 | Tracking Your Business

If you want to stay in business and see your business grow, you can't be lax about this part. This chapter will cover everything from inventory to keeping track of your clients or customers. I know paperwork and bookkeeping may be the last things you want to do, but they are a crucial part of business ownership.

Why do you need to keep track of everything like this? You just want to go to work, sell your quilted items or the kits you've put together, make money on a daily basis, and go home. While everything we talk about in this chapter may seem like a pain, your work life will be a lot simpler in the long run if you keep good records. From keeping an inventory list to keeping up on taxes, knowing where your records are and keeping them up to date will be an added bonus. Let the Internal Revenue Service call you once and you'll be glad you've kept good records.

If things we talk about in this chapter, especially balancing a checkbook or keeping all the tax information straight, is overwhelming, hire an accountant. Most businesses have accountants out of house, and they can be your best ally. They can prepare profit and loss statements, balance the business checkbook, and take care of audits, if that unfortunate event should occur.

Beyond Design

Rita Meyerhoff of Heaven's Quilt's says, "Making my own decisions is great, but having to be an expert on everything is sometimes wearing, especially when the books don't balance and suddenly you are supposed to know how Quicken works and you don't have a clue."

The most important thing is to get started now, at the beginning of your business. It will probably seem tedious and time consuming at first, but over time, you'll get used to it. It will become easier, and you'll get faster at plugging in the numbers, especially if you start out with some nice spreadsheets. Let's get started.

General Business Records

We're going to begin with some easy and general business records that every business needs to have. If you've never worked with any of these items, now is the time to get acquainted with them. You can work with them on the computer or from hard copy. Whichever you use, be consistent. However, if you do decide to start off with physical records, you can always move to electronic later if you think it may be more beneficial.

Client Files or Folders

When you have a client who special orders a quilt or a quilted item, make a folder with the client's name on the tab. You can write the client's contact information somewhere on the inside or outside of the folder. Keep everything in the file: order details, any correspondence with the client, the final invoice, and a copy of the check or credit card receipt when the item has been paid for in full. By doing this, you will be able to pull your notes and see what was done previously if the client ever contacts you again. Having everything in one place will make things go faster.

If you get multiple orders from this client, you can clip or staple orders together as you get them. That way, you will still have one file for the client, and all the orders will be in one place. You can make an electronic file for the client, too, but make sure that everything gets scanned into that file.

Appointment Book or Schedule

You may think you don't need an appointment book or organizer. Think again. The busier you get, the more important this will be to you; as your business grows, you will have more responsibilities and more to think about. You may believe you can remember everything, but you can't—and if you try to, you will wind up forgetting to pay a bill or meet a client who wants to talk about special ordering a quilt. An appointment book is no big deal. You make an appointment and write down the time, name, contact info, and location. Every night before you leave your workspace, check what you have on the agenda for the next day.

Most organizers have calendars. You can choose a week at a glance or a day-to-day space where you can write down your appointments, to-do list, and any notes you need to remember for the day. Most people find it helpful to check off tasks once they are completed so they can feel like they have accomplished something. What doesn't get done on your to-do for one day can be transferred to the next.

Franklin Planners and Daytimers have made their business from helping people keep their lives and businesses organized. If these are too expensive, go to your local office supply store and look at their planners. They always have an impressive selection. Seeing them up close may help you decide which one would work best for you.

Also consider electronic planners and organizers. I like the hard-copy versions, but if you have an iPad or smartphone that will hold a lot of data, electronic might be the way you want to go.

Address Book

Like a planner, an address book is essential for business owners. In the age before electronics, business owners had Rolodexes. Today's business owners are finding smartphones with contact gathering capabilities to be more efficient. You can take a business card, enter the information into your phone, and sync it with your computer when you get home. Your phone uploads the information to your computer's address book/database.

You can also gather business cards, take them home, and scan them into your system. A company called Neat has desktop scanners and portable scanners that allow you to scan your cards and other files. The program then knows automatically where to send and file them. The program allows the computer to collect the information and put it in a database for easy retrieval.

If someone doesn't have a business card, you will need to get that person's name, address, phone/cell phone number, e-mail address, and website (if your contact is a business owner too). You especially want to get your vendors' information. The nice thing about building a database is that you can put searchable words into your information. For instance, if you have five fabric vendors you talk to on a regular basis, you can categorize them as "fabric vendors." You can make a category for customers, fellow quilters, event coordinators, and other types of contacts as well. Once done, you can find these contacts by searching the categories. Let's say you wanted to send out a discount coupon to your customers. You wouldn't want to send it to your vendors, so you would do a search for the "customers" category and send your e-mail to only those people.

Look around. There are many different kinds of programs available today. Find an affordable one that will work for you. You may already have one installed on your computer. All you have to do is learn how to use it.

Forms

In this section we'll be talking about different forms. You may use some of these forms all the time, others once a month, and others only every now and then. Choose what works for you. The most commonly used forms are bid or estimate sheets, invoices, and mileage charts. I've provided samples of each. I've also included a sample machinery maintenance log form and a sample inventory list. You can use these forms as given, or you can take the information and customize it on the computer to fit your needs. You may also find forms you like better on the Internet or at your local office supply store.

While these forms are designed to keep you organized, they can also help you out when tax season rolls around and the Internal Revenue Service is asking for certain information about your business, such as mileage records. Your state may want to see additional information, so make sure you are compliant with all federal, state, and local tax regulations. There's nothing more disruptive to a business than things coming to a halt because you have to deal with tax issues.

As your business grows and your time gets more stretched, you might consider writing form letters that can be used to answer basic questions that arrive via mail or e-mail. You could even write standard sections of a letter, explaining when you started quilting or where you learned to quilt, so that each time someone asks, you don't have to start all over again. The other nice thing about form letters is that you have time to think about what you want to say, edit, and rewrite. Then, when you're finished, you have given a personal touch to your business correspondence.

So let's look at some general ideas for managing various areas of your business and the corresponding forms. Feel free to modify any to meet your needs. Consider these guides to get you started.

Estimate Worksheet

An estimate protects you and your client. When a client comes to you for a bid on a quilt, you will need to know the size of the quilt he or she wants and the preferred fabric so you can estimate the cost. You'll also want to include in your bid the approximate delivery date. If you have made the type of quilt the client wants before, you should have a pretty good idea right away of the cost and the time you'll need. If this is a brand-new project, stress to your client that the estimate you give is just that—only an estimate. It may take more or less time depending on how the designing or sewing goes.

> **To the Point**
>
> When working with a client, you should collect the price of materials up front. You could also work out a deal with your clients. For instance, if they paid you the total on the day of the estimate, you'd give them a 10 percent discount. If it's going to take three months to get the quilt made, you could collect one third the first month, another third the next month, and the remaining balance when you deliver the completed quilt. It's just something to think about, but it makes good business sense.

As an example, let's say you have a pattern and it looks like it will take you ten hours to cut out all the pieces, thirty hours to sew the top together, and then another five to quilt it and get the back on it. That's a total of forty-five hours. If you charge $15 an hour, the total will be around $675 for labor plus what the materials will cost, which could run as high as $300. Don't hesitate to charge this amount, especially for a one-of-a-kind quilt. If this was a quilt you made every day, you would know what to expect, but special orders are different.

See the sample estimate worksheets that follow. Once you work out all your figures, transfer those numbers to the estimate sheet, which is what you will give your client. Again, you can modify these as needed to fit your needs.

Client's name: _____ Date:_____

Project type: _____

Size requested:_____

Pattern requested: _____

Colors requested: _____

COST OF MATERIALS

Color and fabric type	Yardage needed	Price per yard	Total
Misc. items (e.g., thread)			
			Total:

Now estimate how many hours it will take you to complete the project. If you've done this type of quilt before, you should know pretty closely. If not, estimate long. Decide what you are going to charge per hour. Note: If you decide to do a flat fee, like $200 for a baby quilt no matter how long it takes you, just put that number in your total blank.*

_____ hours X $ _____ per hour = total labor cost $_____ *

Add total material cost plus labor cost to come up with estimate. Remember to tell the client that you will add tax and shipping (if any) to the total when the project is complete.

$_____total material cost + $ _____ = total labor cost $ _____

Estimate Sheet

The estimate sheet will be what you give your client once you have worked out the price. This sheet will allow you to write down approximately how much it is going to cost to make a quilt for a customer who wants a custom-made or one-of-a-kind quilt. The nice thing about the estimate sheet: Not only can you rough sketch a design, but you can jot down colors and types of fabric your client wants to use. After you get the price worked out, the client has to sign and date an estimate sheet, showing approval of the project and the price. When clients find anything wrong with the estimate, they will hesitate to sign, giving you the chance to air any concerns. If your client argues with you after the fact, you can pull out the estimate with his or her signature. Usually this stops any lingering debate.

On your estimate sheet, you will want to put your business name, your name, contact information, and the name of your client and the contact information as shown on the next page. You should include a date, description of the job, pricing, and a place for your client to sign and okay the estimate. You can get carbon estimate sheets at your local office supply store or you can print the estimate off your computer, have your client sign in and then make a copy. You will want to keep the original for your records.

Estimate Sheet

DATE: _____ JOB TITLE: _____

Your company name _____   Client's name _____

Address_____   Address _____

City, state, zip _____   City, state, zip_____

Phone number _____   Phone number _____

Website_____   Cell phone _____

E-mail _____   E-mail _____

Project Description	Price
(You can get as in-depth as you need to here. For example you might want to write "72x118-inch, queen-size long cabin quilt made with green, blue, and brown flannel material.")	(Once again, you can list a single price or break it down, putting in material costs, labor, and then your total.)

Estimated date of completion: _____

Comments: (Here you can write down how much your customer paid in advance or any special requests.)_____

_____

_____

_____

_____

I approve and accept this estimate.

Client's signature _____Date: _____

Mileage Chart

You will no doubt be using your vehicle for business-related errands such as going to the fabric store or to a festival where you sell your quilts, or delivering a quilt to the client or post office. Now is the time to get in the habit of writing down your mileage. You should also keep track of how much gas you've purchased, when the oil has been changed, your tire pressure, and more. The Internal Revenue Service won't care about your tire pressure, but it will want to know how much you have driven your car for your business, what you did, and why.

What follows is a sample mileage chart. You can use this one, find a mileage log at your local office supply store, or buy a spiral notebook to keep track. Whichever way you go, just make sure you write down everything. If you don't keep good records, the IRS may disallow some of your expenses, and when it comes tax time, you will want to take off everything you can.

Sample Mileage Chart

Date	Beginning Mileage	Ending Mileage	Miles Driven	Fuel Cost	Turnpike Fees/Tolls	Destination	Reason for Trip
7/30/14	35,689	35,742	53	$10	0	Jane's Fabric Store	Buying material and other supplies for quilt

Machine Maintenance Log

When was the last time you had your sewing machine serviced and for what? Was it the yearly cleaning? Did the belts get changed? If you don't know for sure, then you should be keeping a log of all your machines and business equipment. Most manufacturers will tell you to take your machines in at least once a year for a good cleaning. It is difficult to remember from year to year, so keeping a log is a good business decision.

What follows is a sample maintenance log sheet. I recommend keeping one per machine so that you can track not only when equipment was last serviced, but also the serial numbers and how much you paid for it at time of purchase. If you have more than one machine, you can put your log sheets in a three-ring binder divided by machine, or you can put each one in a separate manila file folder.

Machine Maintenance Log

Machine name _____ Date purchased _____

Serial No. _____ Where purchased _____

Price paid _____ Financed? Yes_____ No _____

Date serviced	Where serviced	What was done	Cost

Keeping the Books

Now, let's move on to an even less enjoyable part of your business—keeping the books. Most business owners dread this because it can be tedious and time consuming, but the bookkeeping has to be done. This includes attention to your business checking account, income and expense sheets, balance sheets, inventory, and more. Let's take a closer look at this and see what all the fuss is about.

First, when you own and run a business, the Internal Revenue Service wants to know how much money you make, where that money goes, and why it goes there. The IRS has strict standards about what someone can call a legitimate business and what is considered a hobby, and they also want to know if the expenses you are claiming are truly for your business or if they are personal. There is a fine line. By keeping good records, you can prove that a business expense you claimed is legitimate. You don't want the agency to throw out a deduction because it is questionable, and they will if you can't prove its legitimacy. And, as you will find out when you run a business, you need every deduction you can get.

Second, you need to keep good records so you can know where your money is going and why. You can't remember everything. Scattered receipts with no notes written on them can leave you scratching your head. You have to know if you are spending your money wisely and helping your business grow or if you are wasting your money on things you don't really need. Besides keeping track of what you are buying, you need to keep track of whom you owe and who owes you. If you don't stay on top of things, you can lose a lot of money.

Because you are small home-based business, record keeping shouldn't be too complicated. You may think it is, but the best piece of advice you will ever receive is to keep it simple. Keep all your records together and stay on top of them monthly. If you let one month slip, things can get out of hand and it can take weeks for you to catch up. Later on, if you decide to expand or hire employees, you will be spending more time on bookkeeping, but for now you will probably spend only about thirty minutes a day and then another two or three hours a month to balance your business checkbook and reconcile all your financial records.

Computers can help with your records if you find the right software. If you go on the Internet and look for bookkeeping software, many times you will find software you can use on a trial basis to see if it will work for you before you purchase. Small businesses have been increasing in popularity, so bookkeeping programs for small businesses are now available at economical prices. One thing, though: If you buy software, learn how to use it—and *use it*. It won't benefit you if you buy it and never open the box.

Programs can speed up your processing time if they do what you need them to do. Think about what you need. You may benefit from building your own charts and records in a spreadsheet program like Microsoft Excel, Apple Numbers for Macs, or Intuit Quickbase. There are other programs available that will allow you to customize and make bookkeeping records *you* need.

If the available choices seem to present too high a learning curve and you're feeling intimidated, you could always consider hiring a professional bookkeeper. You will still have to supply this professional with numbers, so he or she can plug them in where they need to go. A bookkeeper can balance your checkbook, write checks for you, pay employees or bills, and keep track of where your money is going on a monthly basis. It will, of course, cost you, but reducing your anxiety about the whole process might be worth the investment.

Another option is to take bookkeeping classes at a local vocational-technical school or library. Once you learn specific programs, you will probably be able to do the day-to-day bookkeeping yourself and hire an accountant to do the quarterly and year-end bookkeeping. Classes can save you a lot of money in the long run, especially when you compare $220 for a class and $300 monthly for a bookkeeper.

Your Business Bank Account

If you haven't opened a business bank account, do so now. When you are running a business, it is important to keep your business account separate from your personal one. At first, it may seem like an imposition, but in the long run will be well worth it. You need to track what is coming into your business and what is going out. You will get a business checkbook (which is larger than a personal checkbook), ledger, deposit slips, and business debit card. The ledger will allow you to write down what you purchased, where, and for how much. It may cost you a little extra money, but you might want to invest in carbon checks and deposit slips. If you get in a hurry and forget to write down what you bought, where you bought it, and for how much, a carbon copy can be a lifesaver, especially if it's a month later and you are trying to balance your checkbook.

Debit cards come in handy these days. You can use your business debit card to purchase things for your business, but for your business only. This should be a hard and fast rule that you don't deviate from. Another rule is to write down what you purchased as soon as you get home. You will want to keep track of everything you spend, so you don't overdraw your account. If you get cash out of your personal account to pay for business items, write those items down as well and pay yourself back with a business check as soon as possible.

Once a month or once a week, write yourself a check from your business account to pay your salary from the business. You can put that money in your personal account and do anything you want with it. Some business owners don't pay themselves at first. They reinvest their salary in the business. That's fine if that's what you want to do, just remember that doing so can create financial strain later.

When you are opening your business account, look for a bank that doesn't require businesses to keep minimum balances in their accounts. There may be times in the life of your business when you need all the money in your account to pay for bills immediately. If you have to keep a minimum balance of one thousand dollars, neither your bank nor your money is working for you. Try to find a bank too that charges no fees or low fees for businesses. Most free banking is for personal accounts, but some banks will waive certain business fees for a small business that is just starting out. It never hurts to ask.

One more thing to ask about is if the bank is going to hold any of your money for a certain period. It is not unheard of for banks to hold new account funds for up to ten days before you can use them, especially if the amount is one thousand dollars or more. Sometimes banks will hold money if a single check is written for five hundred dollars. If you should happen to get a check for five thousand dollars, know that any bank, regardless of how long you have had your account open, will not release the funds until the check has cleared your client's account, or about ten days. Knowing this in advance can save you a lot of time and hassle. If you know you won't have access to your money, perhaps you can plan differently in those instances.

Balancing Your Business Checkbook

If you decide you are going to do the bookkeeping yourself and use an accountant only when tax season rolls around, the most important thing to do is keep your checkbook balanced and up to date every month. One month of falling behind can be disastrous. By keeping an eye on where your money is coming from and where it is going, you can see if there are any discrepancies that need to be taken care of immediately. One business owner found that his bank had taken out two loan payments in the same month on the same loan. They were hefty amounts, and his other checks would have bounced if he hadn't caught this error. He called the bank, and they were quick to rectify the problem. However, if the business owner had waited, it would have become a bigger mess, especially if his checks were returned or his payments denied.

You no doubt have a personal checking account, so chances are you are a pro at this already, but let's imagine for argument's sake that this is your solo flight. You will need your bank statement and your checkbook ledger. Banks today don't send back the physical checks; instead, they send photocopies of your checks along with your bank statement. Usually they are eight to ten per page, depending on how small they can shrink them. If you do all your banking online and don't receive a hard copy of your statement, which seems to be the trend, you will need to log on and find your bank statement before you begin. The check numbers will be listed in order from lowest check number to highest. The pictures or photocopies of the checks will be the same way.

If you are comparing your bank statement electronically, you might want to save it as a PDF file so you can make some indication on the document that the check or charge has cleared your bank. If you have a hard copy, I suggest you set your ledger to the left, the first page of your statement in the middle, and the photocopies of your checks to the right. Start with the first check. Put a mark beside it on your statement and mark it on your ledger to show it came through your bank. If you are working electronically, draw a line through the check number. You are looking for amounts that have cleared.

As you are doing this, look at the check amount and make sure it agrees with what the bank paid. Sometimes, they will pay an incorrect amount because they can't read the handwriting or because of other common human errors. You might also have transposed numbers in your own record keeping, which can cause headaches. For example, if you write $620 instead of $260, you will mess up your balance. If it should have been $620 instead of $260, you are good, but if it's the other way around, you could have checks bouncing and payments not being made because you thought you had more in your account than you actually did.

In your ledger write down any service charges and automatic debited loan payments that may have come out that month and subtract them from your total. Now that all your checks are marked off, check any debit and ATM charges and mark them off. Finally, make sure your deposit numbers match your ledger and that the deposits you've recorded show up on your bank statement.

Simple Bank Statement Worksheet

Checks Outstanding (Not Taken Out of Bank Account)		Month and Year of This Bank Statement	
Check Number	Check Amount	1. Balance shown on your bank statement	$
	$	2. Deposits not shown (if any)	$
	$	3. Total of bank balance and additional deposits	$
	$	4. Outstanding check total	$
	$	5. Subtract Line 4 from Line 3. Put subtotal here.	$
	$	6. The subtotal is your balance. Write that number here. It should be the same as the number in your checkbook.	$
Outstanding check total	$		

Now it's time to start seeing what works and what doesn't with your statement. If you still get your statements through the mail, there is a form on the last page that will help you calculate your balance. If you can't find one, I've included a simple one above. It works just as well as the one from the bank.

First, you will need to write down the balance the bank shows on your statement. Add any deposits that you've written down in your ledger but that don't show up on your bank statement. Next write down all the outstanding checks and charges that haven't come out of your bank account yet and total them. Subtract the outstanding check amount and any service charges from your statement balance. The amount you end up with should be the same amount in your ledger.

If the amount isn't the same, check your work. Bank statements are generated by computers these days and are rarely wrong. It does happen, but the errors are generally few and far between. Chances are you've made the mistake somewhere in your calculations or have written down the wrong numbers. Go back and check your addition and subtraction. It really is maddening when you are off by pennies, but stay at it. If you let this month slip by without balancing, next month will be worse. Let it go long enough and you could end up bouncing checks, and you don't want that. Service fees for bounced checks alone can run into the hundreds of dollars.

Sometimes you can check and check and still can't figure out what happened. In rare instances, if you can't balance and are off hundreds of dollars, you may have to close down one account and open up a totally new one. Know in advance that this will cost you money. Not only will you not be able to use the checks you currently have, but you'll have to buy new ones. You will also get a new debit card and may have to spend time updating accounts linked to the old account number, so it's better to stay on top of your account. Before deciding to go the new account route, if you have a bookkeeper, have her look at it. She may see something you don't.

Looking at the Nitty-Gritty

Bookkeeping in a small business is fairly simple and straightforward, but there are certain things you *need* to do on a regular basis. You can buy Quicken, Quickbooks, or Peachtree Accounting, which can range in price from forty to four hundred dollars. The higher-priced programs can do more complex tasks, so you'll need to look both at your budget and your bookkeeping needs.

If you're going to be selling products like quilting kits, scissors, and thread or have an inventory of handmade items like baby blankets, bibs, and pot holders, you will want to check out some inventory programs. Inventory Management from NetSuite .com, EZ Small Business, and Quickbooks are good choices, or you can look into the *free* inventory software. These software programs are designed specifically for small businesses. They are simple to use and, unless your business gets huge and you are selling and shipping thousands of items a day, they should work for you. The top-rated ones are POS Maid (POS stands for Point of Sale) at firstmerchantservices.com, Inflow Inventory Free Edition at inflowinventory.com, and ABC Inventory Software at almyta.com/abc_inventory_software.asp.

These programs keep track of what you have in your inventory, allow you to write invoices in the program, and alert you when you start getting low on a particular item in your inventory. For instance, let's say you keep 150 pairs of scissors. You can set these programs to tell you when you reach 25, so you will know when you need to order. Some of these programs even allow you to set automatic ordering when you drop to a specific number of items. Think carefully about using this service, though.

Simple Inventory Worksheet

Month: _____ Year: _____

Product No.	Product Description	How Many on Hand	How Many Ordered	Ordering Price per Piece	Selling Price

**Note: Make the chart as long as you need to cover the number of items you have on hand.

Even though it may seem like a time-saver, if you set it up to automatically order for you and you don't have money in your account to pay for the order, it could become problematic. You may also decide you want to change brands of items you use, or an item may be discontinued. Think of all the ramifications that may come down the pike. If it seems it may cause a hassle in the long run, don't do it.

You can investigate several more free programs by doing a Google search for "free inventory programs." You should play around with several until you find one you are really comfortable with. Remember, they are free, so your search for the right product won't cost you anything but time.

Income

Your income is pretty self-explanatory. Income is the money your business brings in from teaching classes, selling quilts and scissors, and other items. You might want to categorize everything you do so you can see where you are making the most money, but the IRS only cares about the total. On the other hand, if you see quilted baby items bringing in more money than your quilted pot holders, you might want to concentrate on the baby items.

Expenses are a little different because there are two types: variable expenses that vary from month to month and fixed expenses that occur on a regular basis. All expenses should be business related. If they are, then they can be used as deductions when your taxes are figured. If they are personal expenses, the IRS will disregard them as business deductions. For instance, if you and your family go out to dinner, that's a personal expense. However, if you meet a client for dinner to talk about quilting, you meet your accountant for lunch, or you buy lunch at a festival where you are speaking, you can claim all those meals as expenses.

If you are not sure if an expense is business related, talk to your tax accountant. He can tell you right away which ones are valid and which ones are not. You should also be aware that there are some expenses you can claim in their entirety and others you can only take a percentage of. Knowing the difference will help you avoid a lot of trouble in the future.

Patchwork

When you take a business lunch, keep the receipt and write on the back what you were doing and whom you were with. Come tax time, you are never going to remember. For instance, if you are with a client, write that client's name on the back of the receipt and note, "Talked about details of wedding gift project." If you are at a fair or festival, write the name of the festival and what you were doing (e.g., "National Quilting Association: presented workshop on quilt batting").

Expenses

Next, we need to talk about how to keep track of what's going out. The Internal Revenue Service is very picky when it distinguishes between personal and business expenses. If you don't know what it will allow and what it won't, you could get into a lot of tax trouble. In some cases, people have had to do jail time. The best course of action is to know in advance and follow the rules so there are never any questions. It's always a good idea to talk to your accountant if you're uncertain about something.

You may look at this section and think it's overwhelming. Not to worry. We're going to break down some of the different types of expenses so you can be prepared—at least prepared enough to have some idea what to ask your accountant. There are variable expenses and regular expenses that include regular deductions, depreciating deductions, and percentage deductions. We will cover those here.

Variable Expenses

Some expenses may occur all the time in varying amounts, ten dollars one time and five hundred dollars the next. Others may only happen once in the life of your business. A few categories of these on-the-job variable expenses are given below:

- **Materials and supplies.** These are expenses for items you may pick up for a specific job, like specialty thread for a specific quilt. You probably won't have to buy that thread again, so you wouldn't categorize that as a regular expense.
- **Miscellaneous.** These are expenses that fall under no specific category. Use this category until you decide where the expense should go.
- **Labor.** Around the holidays you may need to hire someone to come in and help you. This category should be used to keep track of everything you pay your employees, be they part-time or full-time. Be diligent in tracking these expenses. You will need your reports at the end of the year when working on tax reports.
- **Subcontractor.** These are expenses you will pay out if you use a subcontractor to help you in your business. For instance, if you are overloaded with work and need a quilt finished, you might hire a subcontractor to finish it for you. You would pay just for the one job, and then that person's work would be over. A subcontractor works on a job-by-job basis.

Regular Expenses

These are deductions you know in advance are coming. They may be weekly, monthly, or yearly, but they happen with regularity, and the amount varies only slightly from time to time. That's a good thing. You can prepare for them and, if need be, start saving in advance to pay these expenses before they come due.

Advertising. If you have budgeted for advertising, this is the amount of money you would take out for that expense. Any expense that allows you to get the word out about your business falls into this category: ads in newspapers; fliers for a convention, fair, or festival; business cards; letterhead; estimates; invoices; and your website.

Bank charges and fees. If you have a service charge on your bank account every month, put that expense here. Also, if you are unlucky enough to have bounced check charges on your account, they go here. It's frustrating, but it does happen occasionally. You are in a hurry and transpose a number or forget to record an expense. (Note: If your business account accrues interest, remember to count that as income at the end of the year.)

Business lunches or dinners. Let's say you have a client coming to town who wants to special order a quilt and you recommend meeting at the corner coffee shop. You pay for both your coffees and pastries. Don't throw away the receipt. Keep it because it is deductible. At first, you may think it is a small amount, but these small amounts add up. When it comes tax time, you want to deduct everything you can. Remember, you can take off business lunches and dinners, but you must document what you were doing and whom you were doing it with.

Dues and subscriptions. You no doubt belong to several organizations that charge dues, and you likely subscribe to a number of quilting magazines. The organizational dues and subscription costs can be deducted from your business taxes if they are business related. For example, you can take off a quilting magazine subscription, but you can't take off a women's health magazine unless you have a good reason, such as running ads in it. The same thing goes for organizations. You could take off a quilting organization's dues and even a chamber of commerce expense, but not a membership fee you paid to a knitting club unless you are knitting a blanket that will later be quilted.

Educational fees. If you take any classes to enhance your business, be it business classes for accounting or quilting classes to learn a new quilting technique, keep your receipts. Any classes, workshops, or seminars you pay for that will further your business are tax deductible. You can also claim any books, manuals, or educational CDs you buy for your business as educational fees.

Licenses and permits. When you get your tax permit so you can charge taxes to your customers, you will no doubt pay a fee. Keep track of what you pay. This is deductible as well.

Machine service. When you purchase your sewing or quilting machines, there is a recommended time to take them in for service, be it every six months or once a year. The fee you pay for service on those machines is deductible, so keep track of what you pay along with your receipts.

Office supplies. Anything you might buy to run your office, such as paper, envelopes, tape, staplers, print cartridges, and pens, will fall into this category. As with everything else, keep track of your receipts.

Phone service. If you have a landline or cell phone devoted strictly to your business, you can take the service as a business expense. You can do the same thing for a dedicated fax line if it is for your business and only for your business.

Mailing fees. Because of the nature of your business, chances are you will spend a lot of money and time at the post office, FedEx, and UPS. If you mail out fliers for your business, that's deductible, as is a post office box for your business. You will be charging your customers for shipping and handling. Even though they will be paying you that fee, you need to keep track of what you pay out for shipping. You will want to make sure you keep all mailing receipts, because if you don't have proof to back up what you say you spent for shipping and handling, the Internal Revenue Service will make you claim the difference as income.

Taxes. This category includes any business taxes you may pay such as business property tax, which may include a percentage of your home's property tax, your quarterly business taxes, and more. Keep track of everything you pay.

Your work tools. When you purchase tools like scissors and rulers for your business, keep the receipt. All these items are tax deductible. Items should be kept under a certain dollar amount. If they are not, they will need to be depreciated out (see below) over time. Check with your accountant to find out what the current year's figure is.

Travel and lodging. When you go to a workshop, conference, festival, or fair to speak, teach a workshop, or sell your wares, you can take off travel expenses such as the cost of gas and mileage. If you have to spend the night at a hotel and you are

To the Point

Pay your bills and pay them on time. By keeping your creditors paid and up to date, you will be building not only your business credit, but your reputation. This is important for the future of your business. If you ever want to expand or simply borrow money for another piece of equipment, lenders will look at how well you handled payments in the past. If you get a bad credit reputation, you are going to have a hard time convincing people you can handle credit in the future.

paying, you can take that as a deduction as well. The Internal Revenue Service once again draws a fine line between personal and business, so document, document, document. If you don't, the IRS may throw out your trips as being unrelated to work.

Depreciating Deductions

While we would all like to take off everything we buy for our business right away, the IRS has a different way of seeing things. Depreciating deductions are ones you have to take over the life span of the item you purchased. For instance, if you purchased a sewing machine for five thousand dollars, the IRS wouldn't expect you to go out and buy another one the very next month. So you have to take a percentage of the price you paid over the number of years the IRS views the item as viable to your business. Depreciating items can include computers, printers, sewing machines, and quilting machines, to name a few. The percentage you can take on each item changes from time to time, so make sure you check with your accountant before you purchase equipment. You may not be able to take as much as you think for one piece over another.

Office equipment. This category includes computers, printers, copy machines, fax machines, and anything else office related. The catch is that you must use them for your business and only for your business.

Machines for work. Your sewing machine, serger, quilting machine, and anything else you will be using for quilting will go into this section. If a new piece of equipment comes out that would make your production more efficient and you are not sure if it would be deductible, ask your accountant.

Vehicle. If you use your vehicle for business and only for business, you can deduct the price you paid for it over a number of years. Keep all the papers from when you bought the vehicle, as your accountant will need to separate any taxes and fees that were added when you bought it. Make sure you use it for business or the IRS can also throw out this deduction.

Percentage Deductions

Depending on where your business is located in your home, you may be able to take off a percentage of your monthly house payment for the office and business space you occupy. You will need to figure out how much space you take up and compare that to the total square footage of your home. For instance, if your home is 3,000 square feet and your business takes up 1,000 square feet of that, you would be allowed to claim one third of your house payment as an office and business expense.

You can also take one third of your utilities. Government percentages change all the time, so be sure to check with your accountant to see what the latest regulations are concerning home office and business deductions. Don't overlook these deductions, either; they can add up over time.

Tracking What's Coming to You

While most of your business will probably be cash-and-carry, with people immediately paying for what they buy, if you do special orders you will no doubt have to work with a different system. In this section we'll talk about invoicing, receivables, and balances due.

Invoicing

You will want to work with invoices when doing special-order projects. Why? Because when you get a special order, you should be collecting a certain amount of money up front, and the person for whom you are doing the special order will carry a balance. At the end of the project, you can write on the invoice how much the client has paid and then what the remaining balance will be. Make out the invoice before your client arrives so you can take your time in figuring the numbers. You don't want to short yourself or the client.

When making out the invoice include your business name, contact information, date, and your client's name and contact information. You will also need to include a description of what you did for the client—for example, "design and construct a king-size blanket" or "finish a quilt." Finally, you will need to include the price. If your client has paid in part, write down the amount for the entire project, then write down the amount your client has paid. Subtract what the client has paid from the amount owed and you will have the amount due.

You can find carbon-copy invoice and receipt books at your local office supply store. If you go that route, I suggest you get one with three copies—white, yellow, and pink. The white one would go to your client, yellow to your tax records file, and pink to your customer's file. You can get your business name and information printed on receipts, or you can buy generic pads and purchase a stamp with all the pertinent information. A third option is to make your own invoices and receipts on the computer. You can use the sample invoice that's given here or you can make one that better fits your needs. If you make your own on the computer, once you collect you would print the invoice/receipt, have your customer sign it, stamp it PAID, make a copy for your customer, and you would keep the original copy.

You should write or stamp PAID on every invoice when the customer has paid. If you get paid with a check, write the check number on the invoice as well. Not only does it help you keep track of how you were paid, but your customer can see how the invoice was paid as well. You can get pre-inked PAID stamps in several colors from your local office supply store.

Sample Invoice

Date:	Job Title:
Your company name _____ Address _____ City, state, zip _____ Phone number _____ Website _____ Contact e-mail _____	Client's name _____ Address _____ City, state, zip _____ Phone number _____ E-mail address _____
Job Description	**Price Breakdown** Materials $_____ (You can itemize what you used here or put it in the Job Description box.) Labor (___ hours x $_____) $_____ Shipping $_____ Taxes $_____ Total $_____ Payment 1 $_____ Payment 2 $_____ Total payments $_____
	Balance or total owed: $_____

Accounts Receivable

This section is about money owed to you by clients or customers who haven't paid in full yet. You may not have any outstanding monies due you, depending on the type of business you run. For instance, if your business is cash-and-carry, then you don't have to worry about this. If, however, you work on special orders for clients that will be finished on some future date, you will be owed money in the end.

When you get a special order, make out an invoice, write down the amount the client paid (which should be a third of the total), and then the total the client still owes you. It's a good idea to file invoices in two folders, one labeled "Invoices Due" and another labeled "Invoices Paid." Pocket folders that are closed on three sides are great for filing invoices so they don't fall out and get lost.

Of course, if you are computer savvy, you can do the same thing on a computer. Make file folders for invoices due and invoices paid. Once you have the invoice made, you can save it in the appropriate folder.

These are only a few suggestions. There are other ways of keeping track of accounts receivable. If you have already come up with a system that works for you, by all means, don't change boats in the middle of the stream.

The Bottom Monthly Line

You need to keep track of how much money you are owed using a monthly balance sheet. The following chart may help you keep track. It will allow you to see at a glance how much you have coming in and the number of projects you have outstanding. It also shows how much money you are still owed on projects you are still working on, invoices you have written for new client projects, deposits you have made, and deposits you have checks for but that haven't yet been deposited. After you fill in all the information and numbers, you should have a balance of what you are still owed. This is good if you are doing special orders. You can see where you need to pick up the slack by working more hours on the projects you have or by picking up new ones.

Monthly Balance Sheet

Month of_____ 20_____

Current outstanding invoice totals:	
Brown family heritage quilt ($3,500)	
Stapleton wedding ring quilt ($2,900)	
Tompkins king-size art design ($8,000)	
Robertson baby blanket (gold thread inlaid) ($400)	$14,800
New invoices (1):	
Kifer queen-size cabin quilt ($900)	$900
Subtotal 1	$15,700
Deposits:	
Tompkins king-size art design quilt ($8,000)	
Robertson baby blanket ($400)	
Kifer queen-size cabin quilt ($900)	$9,300
Checks not deposited:	
Brown family heritage ($3,500)	$3,500
Subtotal 2 (Add deposited checks and checks not deposited)	$12,800
Outstanding invoice total (subtract Subtotal 2 from Subtotal 1)	$2,900.00

Tracking What You Pay Out

Whom Do You Owe and How Much?

You also need to keep track of whom you owe, how much you owe them, and what you owe them for. Keep your business bills all in one place so you can grab them in an instant. You may want to pay them all at the beginning of the month or pay some on the first and some on the fifteenth. Like invoices, you could keep two folders—one labeled "Bills Due" and one labeled "Bills Paid." Our banker suggested keeping paid bills in twelve-month folders. Either system will work; whether you want to expand to a bigger system will depend on how many bills you have to pay.

Now that you know where all your bills are, you will need to make some sort of budget chart so you can see everything you owe at a glance. The Bill Balance Chart provided will help you keep everything together. This is only an example. When

Date Bill Received	Biller	Amount Owed	Due Date	Amount Paid	Paid on Date	Balance	How Paid
7/4/16	Jim's Thread Emporium	$214	7/15/16	$100	7/10/16	$114	Ck#4356
7/5/16	B&D's Sewing Machines	$3,600	7/20/16	$175	7/15/16	$3,425	Automatic Debit
7/5/16	GE Financial	$7,345	7/20/16	$200	7/15/16	$7,145	Automatic Debit

making your own chart, you can add columns or increase certain columns as needed. You might want to add a column so you can describe the type of bill it is. There are some columns you will definitely need. For example, include the date the bill was received, whom it was from (biller), amount owed, due date, amount paid, date paid, balance, and how it was paid (by check, debit card, or cash).

Petty Cash

Petty cash is money you take out from your business account to pay for small business items you might not want to pay for by check or debit card. You need to keep track of these just like everything else. You'll want to write down the date, what you purchased, where you purchased it, and the amount. A good rule of thumb is to keep these records monthly so you can see how much you are spending in cash month to month.

You may think it's not a big deal. You take out money and buy things for your business. You buy a pack of needles here for three dollars and a spool of thread for seven

Month of _____ 20_____

Date	Where	What	Amount Paid
7/1	Bank	Check written for petty cash	$100
7/2	Fabric store	Spool of thread and color chart	$12
7/5	Discount store	Lightbulbs for office	$10
7/10	Gas station	Fuel for trip to festival	$50
		Expense total	$72
		Petty cash remaining	$28

dollars there. Make enough of these purchases and they will add up quickly. However, if you don't keep track, the IRS can disallow these expenses.

The chart above can help you get started. You will want to make your chart longer so you can fill in for the entire month, and instead of using generic names like "fabric store," write the specific name of the store you visit. At the end of the month, total your petty-cash expenses and then write down any money you may have remaining.

Summing Things Up

While you may think keeping records is a headache and waste of time, it is as important as any other part of your business. Yes, it may take you some time, especially to get set up in the beginning, but after you get going, you'll become quicker at the process and it will become easier. If you run into problems with certain records or computer programs, remember you can always take classes at local junior colleges, vocational-technical schools, community centers, or sometimes your local library to learn computer programs you aren't familiar with. Check around and you'll find something or someone who can help.

08 Marketing Your Business

In this chapter, we're going to take a look at marketing your business. We'll cover everything from word-of-mouth marketing to developing your website. Marketing is an important ongoing part of your business that may be the difference between failure and success. Besides continually making products, you need to be always putting your business name out in front of potential customers. You shouldn't take this lightly.

As the old saying goes, "You can't sell a product until you have a product to sell." The same holds true for advertising your products. Customers can't buy what you have to sell if they don't know what you are selling. You may be thinking that all you have to do is run a few ads in a local newspaper. This may work for a while, but after you have tapped your local market, you'll want to expand your reach to gain more new customers. This is how your business will grow. Besides, advertising is only a small component of marketing. Marketing encompasses everything you do to draw customers to your business and buy your products and/or services.

You may be shy. Perhaps all you want to do is make your products and sell them. To make your business a success, however, you're going to have to talk about it. "I'm not a salesman," you may say, "and I hate salesmen." That's okay. What you need to do is stop thinking about the sales end of things and simply talk about what you do and share your products. You are in a business where people either will or won't want the product you sell or the services you have to offer. The good thing about your particular type of business is that most of the time you are going to have product to sell people immediately.

In the meantime, let's take a look at changing your perspective on marketing and salesmanship. It really isn't as bad as it seems.

First, get the old salesman stereotype out of your head. Think about when you talk to people about your classes, for instance; you are only offering them a service and giving them the particulars—date, time, and what the class is about. It is then their decision to sign up or not. Think about when you go to a good movie or play. If you enjoy it, you tell your friends where it's showing, how much it cost, and who the actors are without hesitation. You are simply communicating information to people. That's the way you need to look at talking about your business. It's the same concept.

Of course, not everyone you talk to is going to take you up on your offer. That's okay. Salesmen will tell you they typically get a no ten times before they get a yes. Just keep reminding yourself that the more people you reach out to, the better your odds get.

Second, stop thinking of what you're doing as selling. If you make quilts, you are offering people a work of art and a piece of yourself. You could almost consider it a gift, even though you are asking people to pay for what you have made. But think about this. People buy pot holders, quilts, purses, and other items all the time. They buy them for themselves and as gifts, and they typically look for something unique and personal. You have products that fit the bill.

Third, think about marketing as another arm of your business. You may not like to do it and you may go down several dead-end trails before you find an area of marketing that works for you, but it is something you will have to do. And, believe it or not, it will get easier the more you do it.

To be effective with your marketing, just like everything else in your business, you must have a plan. Think about the most effective way of reaching your customers and decide how much you're willing to spend on marketing your business. Other business owners will tell you to plan on using one third of whatever you bring into the business on marketing. While you may have to spend more in the beginning on marketing because of start-up costs, down the road marketing expenses should level off.

You may be thinking you don't know where to start. As you read through this chapter, don't think you have to do everything at once. The best thing to do is get your business cards made and your website up and running. Those two things are the most important. Why? What is the first thing you ask people who start talking about their business? You ask for their business card. Then you ask if they have a website. If people are interested in what you do, they'll want to be able to get in touch with you. Because you will be selling products, they'll want to see what you sell. This can be your short-term marketing plan.

For the long term, think about the marketing suggestions offered in this chapter and then decide which ones you can do in any given month. One or two actions a month is all it takes. For instance, let's say one month you attend a local women's business tea and place an ad in a national quilting magazine. The next month, you may attend a quilting show and craft festival two weeks apart. The following month, you could enter a quilting contest and attend your local quilter's meeting. You might also consider taking one day a week to visit fabric or craft stores in your area.

As mentioned earlier, you don't have to do everything at once. If you can only do one thing a month, then do only one. The point is to take some action to get the word out about your business. It may seem difficult in the beginning, but all this work will produce a snowball effect, and it will gather speed the more you do.

Before you decide on any course of action, let's take a look at some different areas you need to think about when making your marketing plan.

Know Your Competition

You may be thinking another quilt maker is your competition. While that is partly correct, it isn't completely. While there are other people who have quilting businesses, yours is no doubt unique. Maybe you specialize in wedding or baby quilts? Maybe you do family heritage quilts? Maybe you create and design? If you create quality products, have fast and friendly service, and offer what people want, you shouldn't worry about other quilters. In your line of business, people aren't your only adversary. There are other factors in play.

Economy

When the economy gets bad and money gets tight, people hold onto their money and stop buying anything extra. Unless they need a quilt or another item you have made and they have the money for it, chances are they won't be purchasing luxury items. You would do the same thing. If it came down to feeding your family or buying a quilt, which would you choose? People may love your items, but if they can't afford them, chances are they won't buy.

Don't be discouraged if people only take your card and don't buy anything right away. In a tight economy they could be short on cash, or maybe they want to talk later about making something special for someone's upcoming wedding. For two years, I had intended on buying a quilted knitting bag, but every time I saw the lady who sold the bags, I didn't have the money. Finally, I knew she was going to be at a particular festival and put aside money to buy. I wound up buying three from her that day.

Selection

Giving people choices is always a good idea. Perhaps you are at a craft show or quilt festival and you've only brought one item: baby blankets. The people attending may not be interested in baby blankets; they may be more into pot holders or full-size blankets. Of course, you don't know who will be buying what at any given time, but try to take a variety of things with you when you go to shows and festivals. If you find that some items sell consistently well, make sure you always have those items on hand. After a while, you will learn what goes quickly, what you need to bring more of, and what you can discontinue altogether.

Remember too the old saying, "Don't put all your eggs in to one basket." Make sure you have plenty of different kinds of items at different prices so there is something for everyone. Don't make your product line so narrow that people don't have choices.

DIYers

You may be attending an event where people have come to learn how to sew or quilt specific techniques. They might be interested in making quilting products themselves rather than buying finished products.. If you are promoting your classes and selling quilt kits you may make a lot of sales here.

On the flip side, if you are attending a different function and have made kits for people to sew together and quilt, there may be people who don't want to do it themselves and just want a completed product. It will all depend on where you are and what you have to sell.

Other Classes

If you are trying to promote your classes while someone else is trying to promote hers, you might find you are in competition. The other person's classes may not be better or cheaper than yours, but if people are familiar with the other teacher's quilts and reputation, they might opt for her class over yours.

Another obstacle could be location. If you are teaching in a town thirty miles away and the other person is teaching a similar class in the town you are marketing to, students may want to attend classes there. Don't take any of this personally. It's just the way it is. People like convenience, and staying close to home is convenient.

Timing

Another factor of competition is timing. Some months, especially right before winter sets in, you will probably find you sell more quilts. You will probably sell more items in December because of the Christmas rush and in and around June because of wedding season. August or September, on the other hand, may be lean times because people are trying to buy items for school. January is likely to be a slow time too, since people have spent a lot on the holidays and are trying to get back on a budget.

It has nothing to do with you or the items you sell. The timing is just bad. If an area has gone through some kind of disaster and is still trying to recover, that may slow your business down as well. Know that when it's a good time, people will buy. When it's not a good time, people won't. It's as simple as that.

Where to Start Marketing

If you haven't already, the very first thing you need to do is get business cards made. These little gems are your representation when you are not there. They remind people about who you are and what you do. Sometimes customers may like your work and want to purchase from you, but because of time constraints or financial difficulties, may not be able to buy from you right away. If they have your card, however, chances are they will contact you when they are ready.

Don't worry about making your business cards fancy or expensive. They don't need to be. You are conveying information: your name, the name of your business, and contact info (address, phone, e-mail, and website). You can add a small logo, like a quilt design or needles and thread, that conveys what your business is about. Over the years, I'm sure you have picked up a number of business cards. Think about what caught your attention with them. What did you like? What did you dislike?

There are a number of places on the Internet that make business cards. Vistaprint (vistaprint.com) is a popular website because it offers so many options. Using their templates you can just drop in your information. You can also start from scratch and design your own if you know what you want, have a logo you want to use, and have thirty to forty-five minutes to devote to the process. After you have your cards designed, you will have the opportunity to approve your card or make changes before it goes off to the printer. This company runs sales frequently, and it's not unheard of to be able to get 250 business cards for under fifteen dollars, shipping included.

You may be thinking you could save money by making your own business cards. In the long run you won't. I've tried both ways. By the time I went and purchased the cards from the office supply store, got my information centered and where I wanted it on the ten cards to a page, printed them off, and tore them apart, not only was my frustration level high, but I knew it would have been faster, more convenient, more professional looking, and cheaper if I had ordered them from a place like Vistaprint.

Building a Website

The next thing you need to do is get a business website up and running. Today, no entrepreneur can sufficiently operate a business without a website. Personally, I think home-based businesses need websites even more than traditional ones do. When you introduce yourself and your business, people will want to 1) check you and your business out, 2) see what products you sell and your prices, and 3) order when they are ready.

Think of your website as twenty-four/seven exposure to your customers. If you have a website, someone across the country or maybe even across the *world* can be online checking out your products while you sleep. I have to admit, I am somewhat of a website snob and junkie at the same time. If I'm interested in a company, the first place I visit is its website. If the company doesn't have a website, I have a hard time thinking of it as a credible business.

If you don't currently have a website or have never been involved in putting one up, you may feel daunted by the task. Not to worry. These days, there are real-world places you can go to learn about how to build a website, like your local vo-tech school. If you know how to click and drag, there are websites with easy-to-use templates that can help you virtually. It's all a matter of what you are comfortable with. You can also hire companies to build your website, but know beforehand that they will cost a lot of money. If you have a lot of product to sell and are taking credit cards and other forms of payment, you may want to go with the website-building company. Just like everything else, you should get bids and ask exactly what a company can and will do for you.

Don't get overwhelmed with building a website. It takes time. In the next few sections, we'll go over what you need to do to get your website up and running. I've even included a checklist so you can mark off what you've accomplished and what you still need to do (see p. 141).

Your Business URL

If you haven't done so yet, now is the time to buy your Uniform Resource Locator (URL)—or, as it's commonly called, your domain name. You have to have your address before you can start building your website. Ideally, it should be yourbusinessname.com. Because we've talked about business names earlier in the book, I won't belabor the point here except to say that if you can't get a .com URL, try to get a .net. If neither of these is available, rethink your business name. You really want to get a URL with a .com extension because that will alert people that this is a legitimate business.

When you decide on a URL, you'll need to register it. There are currently three well-known Internet domain registry sites: register.com, godaddy.com, and network solutions.com. Prices for registration range from twelve to forty dollars a year, depending on the company you choose. These sites also offer the option to register for more than one year. I recommend registering for up to five years if you can afford it. It saves you a lot of hassle in the long run, and if you have been careful in choosing your business name, you will want to keep it for a long time, anyway.

After you register, you will also have the option to purchase web-building packages from these companies. They typically have templates you can use, or you can go out on your own. If you can't find anything you like with these companies, you might want to check out templates from freetemplates.com, webs.com, and wix. com. You simply find one you like, open your template, and drop or drag in your information. Because you will probably be selling products from your website, you will want to invest in shopping cart software. This makes creating your website a little more challenging, but it can be done.

If you experience trouble building your website or find you have more questions than answers when putting your website together, there are three things you can do, as we discussed earlier. First, you can sign up for classes at your local vo-tech, junior college, or community center. Classes typically run from sixty to two hundred dollars, depending on where you are signing up and what you need help with. Classes could be well worth the price because your second option is to hire a company to build your website, and that can cost anywhere from one thousand to five thousand dollars, depending on what you want done. Third, you can find a computer-savvy teenager to answer your questions or build your website for you. You could also ask around. Perhaps someone in your circle knows someone who has the time, knowledge, and inclination to build your site. Ask for samples of their work and review it much like you would do anyone else you would hire. If you don't like the work they do, move on. Whichever way you decide to go, make sure your website looks professional and reflects your business when completed.

Web Hosting

After you get your URL and you've decided what kind of website you want, you will need to find a company to host it for you. The best way to describe what a web hosting company does is to think of it as a strip mall manager. For instance, if you had a brick-and-mortar business and you found a space in a strip mall, you would pay rent on the space that you leased. The price you'd pay would depend on the size of your store.

When you are looking at hosting companies, be sure to check how much space they allot you and how much it will cost. If they only allow you to build five pages and then start adding extra fees for additional ones, you might want to check around with other hosting companies until you can find one that fits your budget.

Some hosting companies allow you to pay hosting fees once a year, but most will have you pay like you would rent, once a month. Don't confuse this with the payment you have to make on your URL. Your URL will need to be renewed every one, two, or five years, depending on how many years you purchased when you bought your website address. Hosting fees are the monthly charges for space on the Web.

Content

Once you have decided on your name and your hosting company, you need to think about what content you will put on your website. There are a lot of options for content. Below we will talk about different pages you might need for your website and the content you should include. Don't think you have to immediately put a lot of pages up. Most business owners who design their own websites put up a home page, contact information, and maybe another page or two and then build up their sites from there. A quality website takes time, but the good thing about building it yourself is you can make changes whenever you need or want to.

Home Page

So let's look at content. The first thing visitors will see when they visit your website is your home page. On this page, you will want to put a welcome message. You can write a little about your business and what it offers, feature your logo (if you have one), and add a picture or two of what you sell, but the biggest thing you have to get right on this page is your navigation—tabs, buttons, or sidebars. Whichever way you decide to go, you will want to make it easy for your visitor to click through to other pages.

When your navigation system is ready to go, it should connect all the pages you make for your website. For instance, visitors on your contact page should be able to go to a navigation button and click on "home," which would take them back to your home page.

Contact Page

Next, you will want to put up a contact page. This is where you will put your name, e-mail address, phone number, business address, and maybe a suggestion box. Visitors can go to this page on your site and get in contact with you, asking you questions about how to gets bids for quilts, upcoming classes, and everything in between.

Be forewarned, however, that if you do put your email address on your website, you may experience problems with potential spam issues and address theft. There are programs through Google, Yahoo, and Wordpress that can help you eliminate threats by allowing your clients to email you through onsite forms. Your clients' emails will get through to you. Spammers won't.

About You Page

On the about you page, you will want to write something about yourself, when you started sewing and quilting, and why you started your business. You don't have to give out any personal information that you don't want to share; just talk about yourself in general terms. About two hundred words is a good length for your about you page. You want to sound upbeat and excited about your new venture here. Don't say anything negative like "I started my own business because I couldn't get a job anywhere else" or "I started this business because my husband said I should." Say "I started my business because I love working with fabric and wanted to share my designs and craftsmanship with others." This will make a big difference.

Blog

You should probably think about doing a blog on your website. This is a place where you can write weekly, biweekly, or monthly about your insights into the quilting business or craft. A blog is a good place to keep in touch with your visitors. If you post frequently, your visitors will see that you are alive and still doing business. Your blog can offer everything from advice to instruction. If you choose to write weekly, you may want to rotate your topics. One week do a product review, the next week offer a pattern, and the next offer a piece of quilting advice.

Check out sites like simplesite.com, blog.com, wordpress.com, and the most popular blog building site, blogger.com. Once you build your website, you can link to your blog right from your blog page off your website.

Events Page

You can also have an events page. On this page you can list festivals, events, or quilt shows you will be attending and what you will be doing there. Will you be teaching a workshop? Will you have a booth with items for sale? Or will you simply be attending like everyone else? If you will have items for sale at a certain event, you might offer a coupon on this page for anyone who might come by, say hello, and purchase something.

Classes Page

If you offer classes in a certain area, you will want to make a classes page. On this page you can list a description of what you will be teaching, the location, date, time, price, and any items students will need to bring. You will also want to put your contact information again on this page so if people have questions, they can contact you easily. Some of your students may be leery about paying for classes online and will want to mail you a check. If your contact information is readily available, it makes it easier for them to send their class fees to you.

Awards and Recognition Page

You might want to make a page for awards and recognition. If your work has won blue ribbons or if you have been named "Best Quilter of the Decade," you will want people to know about your accomplishments. Not only will this show your visitors that you have a history, but it reassures them about your level of expertise too. You'll want to include the date, title or ribbons won, what for, and who bestowed the honor. A description of the honor would be helpful if it's not evident from the award title itself. If you have fliers or newspaper articles about you or the honor, you might want to scan those in and put them up on this page. This will give you more credibility.

Links Page

One thing website owners do to help drive others to their site is exchange website links with other website owners. You could add a page for this purpose. This will allow you to have a dedicated location to put all the links you gather, and visitors to your page will be able to find similar links that may be of interest to them.

After you add a new link, you could announce it on your main page. "New Link(s)" works well. Curious visitors will go see what you added.

Suggestion Page

Some sites have suggestion pages. Pages like this are typically where visitors can come and leave suggestions for other visitors. Let's say someone found glow-in-the-dark thread and it's the latest trend in Canada. One of your visitors may actually have a handle on when it is coming to the States and where one might go to check out such a product.

Be forewarned about these types of pages, though. You might have visitors who offer an opinion and get irritated if others don't follow their advice. You might also have people who come on to sell their own products. If that works for you, fine, but if that is something you don't want your visitors subjected to, then put a disclaimer on this page saying, "Personal product posts or personal posts defaming, belittling, or causing dissension will be removed immediately, and violators will be banned from posting on the suggestion page."

Website Store

Finally, there is your website store. If you are making a website to sell items, you definitely want a store. On this page you will list all your items, their dimensions if applicable, price, and how many of these items you have available. Listing how many of the items you have for sale in each category will keep your customers from becoming frustrated if something sells out. If you don't quantify on your website, they may think there are plenty of these items and put off buying them when there may only be one in stock.

When thinking about building your store, you will need to consider storage space, site design, and safety protocols. How many items you will be selling should determine your storage space. You don't want to have to pay for something you don't need. However, at the same time, you don't want to run out of room if you ever think about expanding.

Next, consider site design. Will it be user friendly? Will your customers be able to easily navigate the site and buy your products? We've all been on websites where it becomes more trouble than it's worth to buy an item.

And then there are site safety protocols. This is the biggie—more important than anything else, I would say. Make sure the program you use has SSL (Secure Socket

Layer) encryption. You can recognize it by the little lock icon. If you are looking at a program that doesn't have this feature, look elsewhere. The fastest way to ruin your business is to have your customer's information stolen.

To find a store program that may work for you, check out top100onlinestore builders.com. This website has listed ten of the top sites that can help you build your own store. Check out each one listed to see what will work for you, as they each have different options. Monthly pricing fees vary and some charge start-up fees, but most offer two-week to one-month free trials. Some allow you to take PayPal in addition to credit cards, while others have coupon functions, social integration, and reporting and analysis tools.

Another site you might want to investigate is intuit.com. If you already know what you want to put in your store and how you want to build it, this company might be the one to use. Intuit can also help you build a site and get you started accepting credit cards as well.

Another option is to go on etsy.com, open a store there, and then link to it from your website. So you would have a "store" tab or button on your website, and when visitors clicked on it, they would go directly to your Etsy site. You can actually do the same with all the companies you investigate; you will just have to figure out which one has the best security and best prices.

Website Content Checklist

- ❏ Home
- ❏ Contact page
- ❏ Blog
- ❏ Store
- ❏ About you
- ❏ Events
- ❏ Classes
- ❏ Awards and recognition
- ❏ Suggestions
- ❏ Links

- ❏ Name chosen for website
- ❏ Website URL name registered
- ❏ Hosting site chosen
- ❏ Layout and design chosen
- ❏ Background and history written
- ❏ Contact information included
- ❏ Business description written
- ❏ Contact page completed
- ❏ Content store designed and functional
- ❏ Go live

Updating Your Site

Once you get your site built and you go live, updating it should be pretty simple. You will want to check the total contents of your site at least once a month and make sure everything is up to date. Of course, if you have a blog, you will be updating it once a month or every couple of weeks. You could plan to check the rest of your site then. At this time, you might also want to post special offers or coupons.

It's a good idea to set a date and put it on your calendar. Then, on that date every month, update your site. Try to add something new, like a new product, pattern, or product review. Besides giving your customers something new to look at every month, search engines will be able to find you more easily.

Marketing Your Website Online

Now that you have your website built, you will want to make sure people out there in cyberspace know of its existence. The easiest way for that to happen is for you to get your URL listed in some online directories. Back in the old days, businesses would make sure to get their business listed in the Yellow Pages. Consider these online directories the modern, up-to-date, new and improved Yellow Pages. With these Internet directories, people can find you more easily than ever before. As smartphones become more commonplace, people (especially in the younger generations) are using them more to find information quickly and bookmark it on their phones for later use. Being listed in any online directory is a smart and savvy business move.

Getting Your URL on Business Directories

Today, there are all kinds of business directories listed on the web. Some charge you and some are free. Some list free small businesses and then will charge large corporations. You will have to seek out the ones that will do you the most good. There are directions on each site about what and how to list. On some sites, you will want to find specific categories to put your business in to make it easier for your customers to find you. For instance, people will be able to find you more easily if you are listed under "quilting" or "sewing" than if you are listed under broader categories like "crafts" or "weddings."

There are millions of directories out there. If you do a Google search, you will get more than twelve million hits. Among these hits, however, are some good directories and some not-so-good ones. Below is a list of the most well known:

atlist.org
businessdirectory.bizjournals.com/claim/add
dexknows.com
www.google.com/+/business/manta.com
merchantcircle.com/signup
ubl.org
yellowpages.com
yelp.com

Local Directories

You will also want to get listed in some local directories. These directories allow people in your general area to find you. When you visit the sites listed below, look at your competition and see what you can add to your listing that will grab someone's attention. Sometimes local directories will let you include comments or reviews of what customers have said about your business. Don't pass up this opportunity. If you have a review or kudos, include it in your listing if it is allowed.

Below are seven of the more frequented local directories:

citysearch.com
insiderpages.com
local.com
local.yahoo.com
showmelocal.com/businessregistration.aspx
thewebmap.com

Association Directories

Because you have a small business, you will also need to join and get listed in some association directories. A good place to start is with your local chamber of commerce and small business association. These organizations will often list members and their businesses for free, and sometimes they even publish a front-page article introducing you to the community. Take advantage of these organizations, as their role is to help your business grow.

You probably belong to at least one quilting, sewing, or fabric organization. If you don't, go out and join at least one or two. When you join, make sure your information is correct and keep it up to date. A directory listing won't help you if customers don't know where to find you. Typically, if you need to make changes to your listing, all you have to do is notify the organization and it will make the changes for you.

Besides joining your local chamber of commerce, below are three other organizations you should look into joining:

The National Quilting Association, nqaquilts.org
American Quilter's Society, americanquilter.com
International Quilt Association, quilts.org

Joining a Forum

Most of the quilting organization sites have forums. Forums are places where you can post comments (tips, suggestions, patterns, etc.) within threads. Everything discussed in a thread is related to one topic or theme. For instance, there may be a new pattern circulating. Perhaps the pattern has problems and everyone is talking about those problems in a particular thread. People will be posting what they've tried that works with this pattern, and others will be asking questions about what they can do about problems they are facing with it. The designer of the pattern may show up and clarify any questions or offer suggestions herself.

There are millions of quilting forums on the Internet. Start by checking to see if the quilting groups you belong to online have forums. Many of them will. You can also do a Google search for "quilting forums" and find a forum that works for you.

Joining a forum is a great way to get your name and the name of your business out to the public. When people get to know you, not only will they start visiting your site, they will also tell others about you and your business.

Exchanging Links

Just like networking in real life, you will need to get on the Web and start networking with others who have quilting businesses on the Internet by exchanging links. For instance, if you visit a website that sells fabric, contact the owner of the site to say that you will add the owner's URL link to your site if he or she will add yours. The more websites you exchange with and the more hits both of you get, the more word will get out about both of your sites.

When you get an okay from the other person, add that link to your website in a timely manner. You might want to give a small description of the site so that people know what they are visiting. As suggested under Building a Website, consider making a "Links" page where you can add all the websites you have traded links with. That way you can keep them all organized and in one place. You can make an announcement on your home page when you have added a new link.

Building an E-mail List

You may not have thought of having an e-mail list. If you haven't, now is the time to not only stop and think about it, but get started. An e-mail list can benefit you in a number of ways. You can keep track of your customers and e-mail them when you have sales or when something new and exciting is happening with your business. Because you have everything stored in one place, getting in touch with clients, customers, vendors, and others becomes a lot easier and more convenient for you.

Another advantage to having an e-mail list is that you can send out mass e-mails to certain groups of people instead of having to send out individual e-mails one at a time. When gathering your information and building your database, add tags to people like "customers," "vendors," "friends," and "classes." When you get ready to send out newsletters, coupons, or class announcements, you can go into your database, sort for the group you want to e-mail to, and send your information to that group only.

If you don't have a customer's or vendor's e-mail address yet, don't worry. All you have to do is ask. Most people are more willing to give you their e-mail address than their phone number because when they get an e-mail, they can take their time reading it or delete it if they are not interested.

You don't have to send out an e-mail or newsletter every month, but you should try to keep in touch with your list and send out something at least once every three months. This will keep your business name in front of your subscribers and, if you are offering specials, drive them back to your website. If you hit some slow months, you might want to send out monthly e-mails reminding people about your store and what you have for sale.

Probably the easiest and least intrusive way to get people's e-mail is to allow people to sign up for newsletters, coupons, and other information on your website. When you get their information, put it in your database. As you are sending out your e-mails, make sure to include an "opt-out" option for people who decide they don't want to get e-mails from you on a regular basis. You will want to be respectful of your customers' and clients' privacy. You should keep any information you collect—such as e-mails, phone numbers, addresses—to yourself. Don't give out a customer's information, don't sell it, and don't use it for anything other than what it was gathered for—to share information about your business. Trust is a fragile thing in today's society. Don't lose your customers'.

Social Networking

Besides networking face to face, you will also want to spend some time networking online. On any given day you can find thousands, if not millions, of people online talking about what is happening across the globe. The topic of conversation ranges from politics to the hottest new shoe trends. You might as well get on and get people talking about your business as well.

The most popular social networking sites are Facebook, Twitter, and LinkedIn. Once you join these sites, friends, colleagues, and business associates can follow you. Anything you post will be read by, for instance, all your "friends" on Facebook. And your friends list can grow quite quickly, because once someone signs on to follow you, that person's friends may follow you too if they have similar interests. You can go from ten followers to five hundred or more in a month or two depending on how often you use the site.

Word, good and bad, travels quickly through social media. If you want to spread any news quickly, log on, post a message, and send it out to the mass audience. If your content is interesting, one person will send it to another, who will then send it to someone else, and that person will send it on to his or her list of friends. A word of warning here though: Be careful what you say on the social networks. When you post, your posts will reach *all* your followers. If you gossip or say something negative about someone, I can guarantee that, in time, it will come back to bite you in the keister.

Because you are starting your business, you should belong to at least one social networking site, if not two. These sites will take up some of your time, but the contacts you make may be what you need to jumpstart your business. There are advantages and disadvantages to each social networking site. Take your time and investigate the different ones until you find one that will work for you. Below are seven of the most popular at this time:

facebook.com
instagram.com
linkedin.com
pinterest.com
tumblr.com
twitter.com
youtube.com

To the Point

If you have signed up for multiple networking sites but find you don't have time to visit them all on a regular basis, check out Constant Contact, constantcontact.com. This company has a program that allows you to write one message and send it to all your social networking sites. You can even adjust your options so your message goes to your e-mail list as well.

You don't have to go with any of these seven sites. There are others out there. You can go on Google, do a search for "social networking" and find many, many more. While Facebook and Twitter are big at the moment, at any given time another social network could spring up and eclipse these two. Networking sites come and go. Keep up on the trends and change as you need to for the sake of your business. If you are hesitant to join a social network, at least try it once. You never know whom you will meet out there, and any exposure for your business is a good thing.

Social Networking Etiquette

Networking on the Web has its advantages and disadvantages. One advantage is that instead of sending out multiple e-mails when you go on a social networking site like Twitter or Facebook, you write a message once and it goes to everyone who follows you. A disadvantage is that if you send out the wrong message, it's still going to go to everyone who follows you. You are trying to build your business, so you don't want to offend anyone with anything you say, much like when you are having a conversation in person. While there are no hard and fast rules to networking online, below are a few suggestions to protect yourself and your family and gain followers and keep them rather than having them ignore you.

Don't ramble.

When you post a message, get to the point. There is no need to tell everyone in minute details about your day, how it went, and what you intend to do for the rest of the day. No one cares. Say what you need to say and move on. I love Twitter for this very reason. Twitter only allows you 140 characters including punctuation. Once your characters are up, you can't post any more in that particular message. This keeps people from rambling.

Don't post negative comments.

Social networking is not the venue for you to vent about your life, acquaintances, or other business associates. We used to live in a small world. The Internet has made that world a lot smaller. News travels fast on the electronic highway, and if you post something negative about a customer, quilting competitor, or vendor, word will eventually get back around to that person. If you are having problems, vent your frustration anywhere but on your social networking sites. Once you send your comments out into cyberspace, they're out there. You can't get them back.

This can be a double-edged sword for you. First, when the person you are writing about reads your comments, he or she will become frustrated and possibly write something negative about you. If your potential clients and customers read something negative you wrote about someone, they may wonder what you will write about them and avoid you altogether. Therefore, social networking sites are not the place to argue or fight.

With that said, if someone comes on and asks your opinion about a product or another business, say, "This is what happened to me . . ." Social networking sites also offer private messaging options. If you have a lot of negative experiences to offer, you can take it off the boards and write a private message to someone, allowing only that person to see your comments.

Don't post personal information.

It's sad that we live in a world where we have to watch everything we do and say, but that's our reality. We've all heard stories about people stealing identities, robbing people, stalking, and even killing family members. You may think it would never happen to you. The truth is, though, you can't be sure. With that in mind, when you post, don't disclose your Social Security number, the year or place you were born, your family members' names, if you are going on vacation or to a funeral, if you are alone, or any other information that criminals might exploit.

Don't send spam.

When people sign up to read your blog or add you to their social network list, they are expecting something. In this case, they are following what you say because they are they interested in the quilting business, products you make, or perhaps some specials you may be running. Don't violate that trust by talking about something your readers aren't interested in or, worse yet, inviting them to play games or visit Farmville. Don't forward information unless it is a really good deal related to your area of expertise and you think your readers might like to get in on it too. You are a quilting business, so people might appreciate your posting about a close-out sale on fabric at an online store. They probably won't appreciate it if you post about the latest fashion jewelry sale.

Be polite.

Hopefully, our mothers taught us manners. It would be wise to use those same rules on the Internet. Rudeness, inappropriate language, and personal attacks should not be tolerated on any of the social media networks. People have bad days, but if someone says something that makes you angry, don't respond in an unprofessional way. If you can't say anything nice, don't respond. At the very least, walk away and give yourself time to think of an appropriate response. When you do respond, be diplomatic. Your business will not benefit from your being rude.

Stay on topic if you are on a forum.

You always want to stay on topic, which means talking about quilting and your business. When you join a forum and post there, you will want to stay on topic within the particular thread. For instance, let's say you are on the Quilters Club of America forum and one of the groups is talking about cutting out patterns. Don't go in and start talking about finishing techniques. This thread is for cutting out quilt patterns. If you want to talk about finishing techniques, start another thread.

Be helpful, not critical.

When you join a group, the best thing you can do is be helpful and not critical. Some people are already shy about asking questions. You will probably be asked the same questions over and over again. If so, try to have some patience. This person may be new to the thread and didn't read your earlier response posted over a month ago.

If someone has posted a problem about a project, a pattern, or a machine, try to help that person find solutions. Sometimes the problems may seem silly to you, but telling someone that or that what they tried was the stupidest thing anybody could have done will not help the situation. Offer suggestions. You might say something like, "Next time, why don't you try . . ." Everybody asks their share of stupid questions, but if you can offer a suggestion without making the person feel smaller than an ant, you will win over a potential customer.

Networking Face to Face

Now that you have your business cards and your website up and running, it's time to go "back to reality" with your networking. This means meeting people face to face and building relationships with them with the intent of building your business. Don't feel squeamish about this process. Everyone does it, and those who are good at it grow successful businesses.

Through networking you talk to people about what you do in your business. You'll ask them about their businesses, exchange business cards, and move on. It may seem in the beginning that not many people are interested in what you do, but don't despair. People will eventually talk and spread the word. The more you are out in the community talking about your business, the more people will know about it. You may have to spend a couple hundred dollars joining organizations, but it will be worth it when you start getting leads and people start calling or ordering from your website.

Patchwork

"When I started, I did the logical thing," Betty of Betsy's Quilts says. "I advertised in newspapers, magazines, and on the radio. But I learned the best way of advertising is word of mouth."

Don't expect to network once and then quit. Networking is an ongoing process. You have to do it week after week, month after month. Building your business through networking takes time, but the more you talk to people and the more often they see you, the more likely they will remember you and pass your name on to others and use your services. This type of marketing takes time. Someone may need your services right away, or it may be six months to a year before someone contacts you. If you believe in yourself, what you are doing, and your business, you'll be fine. Don't get discouraged. Persistence is the key with any endeavor.

Below are some tips to help you get started and on the right path when you network.

Network productively.

When you first start networking, go to meetings where you will meet lots of people, particularly women. It's not that men won't be interested in your business, but women may be more receptive. If there is a Women's Small Business Association, quilt guild, or sewing organization in your area, this would be a good place to start. Attend group meetings a few times and see if they are beneficial to you. If they aren't, then find another group. Your local chamber of commerce is another good group to join. They typically have quite a number of men and women from the local community in attendance. Remember, the more people you meet, the more potential clients you will have.

Attend meetings regularly.

Usually groups meet once a month. At first, this may seem like a hardship, but you need to get your name and face out in front of people. If you only attend one meeting a year—say, the annual organization picnic—people will forget about you. They may even think you died or moved out of town, as has happened with other business owners in the past.

Get involved.

Serve on the organization's committees or board. You don't have to be president of the organization, but if you help with the annual charity drive or organize the annual Christmas bazaar, you'll be involved with the organization and people will start to know who you are.

Arrive early to meetings and leave late.

This doesn't mean you have to be the first one there and the last one to leave, but most networking opportunities happen before or after the meeting. It's difficult to network while the group is discussing business or when someone is giving a presentation. Ten to fifteen minutes before and after the meeting is ideal. This allows you time to say hello to members you already know and meet new ones you haven't spoken with before.

Meet new people.

Don't stagnate and continue to talk to the same people you've talked to before. Sure, this will feel comfortable to you, but stretch your boundaries and talk to new people—new to the group or just new to you. At first, this may feel intimidating, but the more you do it, the easier it will become.

Carry an ample supply of business cards.

By now, I hope you have made it a habit to carry your business cards with you at all times. In a networking situation, not only do you need to have them on hand, but you need to have plenty with you. A good rule of thumb is to always have twenty-five with you when you attend networking events. Don't be shy about passing them out, either.

When you pass yours out, chances are a business owner will reciprocate and give you one of his or hers. Collect all the cards you can. You can add all these members to your contact list. On the back of the card, you might want to write notes like where you met the person. Maybe she mentioned she knew your brother or a good friend of yours. Maybe he told you that his wife was sick or that he had a son in the military. By writing such notes on the back of the cards you collect, you'll remember the person you talked to. You will also make a good impression the next time you meet and you remember to ask how that wife or son is doing. That new contact will be touched you remembered.

Wear your name tag.

Most people don't care for name tags, but in networking situations they are essential. Write your first and last name and the name of your business on your tag. Wear it on the right side so that when people meet you and shake your hand, they can see it easily.

Don't wait to be approached.

The worst thing you can do is stand on the sidelines and wait for people to come to you when you are at a networking opportunity. Don't be rude and interrupt a conversation; there will be plenty of opportunity for you to walk up to someone and introduce yourself. Do it.

You may think you are shy and that keeping to yourself is just how you are. Others may not see it that way. They may think that you think you're better than they are or that you see them as unimportant. The best way to draw people in is to go up, introduce yourself and ask them what kind of business they have. Here are some other questions you can ask:

- How long have you belonged to this group?
- What drew you to this group?
- Do you know tonight's speaker?
- How long have you had your business?
- Where is your business located?

People love to talk about themselves. If you get them to open up to you about themselves, they will become equally interested in you. That is how networking works and how relationships are formed and built.

Finding Networking Opportunities

You may think there are limits to where you can network. That is not true at all. Because all networking involves is opening your mouth and talking about your business, networking opportunities exist all around you. Below are some networking suggestions for you to consider.

Talk to friends and relatives.

Because you already have a relationship with these people, it should be easy for you to talk to them about your business. Talking about your business is networking no matter whom you are talking to. A word of caution, though: Don't talk about your business incessantly. It can drive people crazy if that's *all* you talk about. You have other interests. You did before you started your business, and you still do now. As a business owner, you walk a fine line. You want your relatives and friends to know what you do, but you don't want to drive them away, either.

Informal networking.

This type of networking can be done anywhere, anytime. You might meet someone at the supermarket, library, or at church. Sometimes you'll be asked what you do. Be ready to tell the person who asked and give your business card. You don't have to be overbearing; just casually let people know.

Quilt shows and festivals.

It may take you some time to get into one of these events, but once you do, the time and effort will have been well worth it. Thousands of people typically pass through quilt shows and festivals. People from all over the country tend to show up because they want to see what's new in the industry.

It's not cheap to get a booth at one of these events. They average between five hundred and two thousand dollars for a three-day event. There may also be a waiting list of two to three years, so the sooner you get your name in front of the event's coordinators, the better. The coordinators will put your name on a list and contact you when a spot opens up. The price of getting in is only for your spot. You will have to provide banners, signs, and anything else you need to draw people to your booth.

Before you get in, you need to give some thought to what your purpose will be. Will you have items to sell? If so, you need to make sure you have enough items to sell to recoup your expenses. When people attend events such as these, many will be looking for bargains. While people may like what you do, if they can't afford what you have to sell they'll pass you by. Consider making and taking big-ticket items as well as smaller, more affordable pieces. That way everyone leaves happy and you make some money.

Also consider putting out your business cards and maybe offer specials on your website to people who mention they stopped by your booth. You can also offer freebies like pencils, rulers, or pens with your business name on them to draw people to your booth. A lot of people will come by to pick up the freebies, and when they do, they will also get your name, business name, and website.

Join organizations.

Join as many organizations that will benefit you as you can afford. These are a great place to get the word out about your business. You can join national quilting organizations first and then local quilting guilds. But don't overlook local chambers, women's organizations, and any other community groups available to you. These groups network for their members. They may feature you on the front page of their newsletters or put you up on the front page of their websites with a link to yours.

Teach a class or give a demonstration.

Another good way to get your name out into the community is to teach a class at a local fabric store or a place that sells sewing machines. You could also contact the women's clubs in your area, rotary groups, senior citizen centers, garden clubs, Girl Scout groups, 4-H, or family clubs. These groups are always looking for qualified people to come and share their knowledge. You might be able to do a presentation on the history of quilting or quilting through the ages. If you have a special way of cutting out patterns or special hand-sewn quilting techniques, you could also offer to give demonstrations. You will have to ask around to find where you might be wanted, but once you get your foot in the door, chances are people will contact you.

Volunteer or donate.

From going into a location and showing people how to sew to sewing and donating quilts to worthy causes, volunteering can get your business name out into the public. When you volunteer, many times the organization you are volunteering for will make sure to mention your services. They may put your name on a placard or run a list of volunteers in the local newspaper or organization newsletter. Donating can offer you the same exposure.

If you are stretched for time, offering to donate a quilt a year might be the way to go. You can let an organization know you will donate one quilt a year and then chip away at it all year. You can also suggest that the group take the quilt and auction it off if you would prefer that method of donation.

Whichever way you decide to go, don't overlook donating products or your time. You will meet other people when you do this and you never know where that will lead.

Publicity

So far, we've been talking about what you can do to market your business in person or virtually. Now let's talk about some behind-the-scenes things you can do to get your business out to the public. First, you need to understand the difference between publicity and advertising. The major difference is publicity is free, while advertising is generally something you pay for.

To keep your name in front of the public, you might want to think about sending out press releases regularly. Of course, you will have to vary the information you include in your press releases, but that is easy to do. Let's say you've sent in a release about your business being new to town and you've sent in information about the latest prize one of your quilts won. Why not write a press release about the organization to which you're donating a quilt? If the fair is coming to town or to a town nearby, you could write an article about the history of quilting as pertains to this particular fair. You may consider this to be a waste of time, but, believe me, it is not. All it will cost is a little bit of your time, and it can lead to your being considered an expert in the field.

If you are moaning and groaning about writing a press release, don't worry about them. Press releases are easy to write. If you hire someone to write one or more for you, it will run you hundreds of dollars, so you might as well try your hand at them. You don't have to be a writer, and you don't have to make it fancy. Just stick to the basics and you'll be fine. On the next page is a standard press release. Set yours up a similar way and plug in the information about your business. Get a few under your belt and you'll wonder what you were afraid of. You can also look for press release examples online if this one isn't enough to make you feel comfortable writing them.

To get publicity, you will have to contact local newspapers, television channels, and radio stations with a press release that shows why your business is newsworthy. "How is my business newsworthy?" you may ask. If your business is new to town, you are newsworthy. If you have won a blue ribbon at a local fair or festival, that's newsworthy. Newspapers, especially the smaller community papers, like to announce new businesses to the community and to run articles on hometown people who have achieved success."

Your Company Name

Your Contact Information

FOR IMMEDIATE RELEASE

Headline or Title (e.g., Quilting Business in Town Promises to Keep Customers Warm while Stylish)

City, State, and Date (Month, Day, and Year). Your opening goes here. It will consist of the who, what, when, where, and why. If you get stumped, simply ask yourself the questions. Who is this press release about? What is it about? For example: "Earlier this fall, Betsy Smith opened her quilting business, Betsy's Designs. On Thursday, November 12, 2014, at 3:00 p.m., she will be presenting some of her designs at the school holiday bazaar. You can stop by, see her work, and contribute to a great cause at the same time."

The body of your press release should consist of no more than four to five paragraphs, and the entire release shouldn't run over a page. Spend most of your time working on the opening, as that will be the part of the release that will cause the reader to go farther or stop. The remaining paragraphs will be an extension of your opening. Think about a press release as an upside-down funnel. You want all your important information at the beginning. The remaining paragraphs will support the first one.

Reserve the final paragraph to tell a little bit about you and your company in two or three sentences. For instance, you can write, "Betsy has an online presence but is more than happy to welcome customers into her shop, where they can buy one of her already-made quilts or talk to her about doing a special design quilt. She has been quilting for more than twenty years and makes everything from baby bibs to designer king-size quilts."

At the end of the release, put the following contact information:

Contact: Betsy Smith

Phone Number

E-mail Address

At the very bottom of your page, you need to center and type END or use ### to indicate your press release is finished.

###

Where most people go wrong with press releases is sending them to the wrong person. If they don't get in the right hands, they are often discarded or left to float around from desk to desk until someone finally picks them up, reads them, and considers the information. If you are sending a press release to a newspaper, magazine, or newsletter, send it to the editor or managing editor of the publication. Station managers handle television and radio press releases. If you are not sure where to direct your press release, call the media outlets and ask. They will give you the correct names and locations. Keep track of this information because you can use it in the future.

Photos

If you haven't given any thought to photos, you should because they can enhance any advertising you do. You will definitely want to put photos on your website. You no doubt will be taking pictures of the products you sell. Any product pictures you take can be used on your website and in your marketing scheme as well.

Besides pictures of your products and projects, you'll want to get a headshot taken of yourself. You should go to a professional to have your headshot taken and make sure to get digital copies of your prints. Today, digital images are used more often than prints because they are so easy to attach in an e-mail. If newspapers ask for a picture of you, they will want a digital or electronic version. You can scan hard copies in and send them, but they can lose some clarity and definition during scanning.

You can take the other pictures you use yourself—you can use your smart phone, smart tablet, or a good point and shoot camera. All these are acceptable and should produce enough good pictures for your website. You also might want to invest in a DSLR (digital single-lens reflex) camera. Canon, Nikon, and Sony typically have some very good DSLRs that won't break your budget. They aren't cheap, but they aren't mind-blowingly expensive either. You don't have to buy the most expensive one, but don't buy the cheapest either. A mid-range price is always good; if you take care of it, the camera should last you a long time. Before you buy, do some homework. Visit digitalcamerainfo.com to compare prices, check ratings, and see digital camera specifications.

Once you get your camera, you might want to check with the local vocational-technical school or community center and see if they offer photography classes. You might not think you need any help, but learning how to stage your products, and knowing about light variables, aperture, and shutter speed can make quite a difference. At the very least, go to the library and get a book on taking pictures or check your favorite bookstore for books like *Digital Photography* by Darren Rowland, *Understanding Exposure* by Bryan Peterson, and *Photography for Dummies* by Russell Hart. You can also check out other "Dummies" series books because they also have guides for operating specific cameras.

Once you have your pictures, you can use them in your advertising as well. One important note: Be aware that photographers own the copyright to the photos they take, so to avoid problems be sure you discuss upfront your plans for the photos you're purchasing. You don't want to get headshots and then not be able to use them.

Advertising

As I mentioned earlier, advertising is a part of marketing that you pay for. Most people think of advertising before they think of publicity, and it should be the other way around. Depending on what type of advertising you choose to do, it can add up quickly and drain your bank account.

Before jumping in and spending a lot of money, take the time to think about your marketing plan. How much have you budgeted for advertising? How much time are you willing to spend to make sure your advertising pays off? Will your ads reach the people you want to reach? Have you done everything you can do outside of advertising to reach your potential customers? And, finally, can your advertising attempts rival your competition's? In other words, what's going to make your advertising stick out?

When considering the time factor of advertising, don't think about running just one ad and calling it good. Advertising professionals will tell you it takes time for people to even notice your ad, and even if they notice it, it takes twice as long for them to act on it. Like networking, you have to keep your name out in front of people to make a difference. It takes time to see results. You just have to be patient and be in it for the long haul.

So check prices and figure up your budget to see if it will pay for you to advertise. If you don't think the sacrifice to your budget will be worth the rewards, then try something else before sinking your money into a 2 x 2 ad. An 8½ x 11 trifold color brochure may sound nice, but if you don't have that much information to include or you don't have a large audience to reach, spending two thousand dollars for five hundred brochures isn't very economical. You can put information on the front and back of a single panel (8½ x 3⅔), and that may be all you need. Think about where you are going to get the most benefit for your dollar.

Business Ads

If you think this type of advertising would benefit you, you can create an ad to run in local newspapers or magazines. These advertising outlets typically charge by the inch, so check out the prices. For instance, a 1 x 3 ad may run you seventy-five dollars, while a 2 x 5 ad may cost three hundred dollars. You will also be charged extra for color. Prices will vary not only by size, but also by frequency. For instance, a magazine may charge you seventy-five dollars the first time you run your ad and fifty dollars each time you run it thereafter. This also depends on whether you run the ad for consecutive weeks. If you pull the ad, you'll have to start over at the original price next time you run it. You can call the publications' marketing or advertising departments to get quotes and requirements for their ads. Don't be hesitant about calling—businesses call them all the time, so they are used to it. Publications can also fax or e-mail you a written estimate after you've spoken. It's always wise to get the quote in writing.

When thinking about running ads, consider the audience the publication reaches. You wouldn't want to advertise in an auto magazine, because men who are interested in cars aren't likely to be interested in your quilting products unless you make car-themed quilts. You don't have to go with the high-priced newspapers in your area or the expensive magazines. Small community newspapers will offer you better pricing and more space for that price. As far as magazines go, sometimes you can get a small ad in the back of publications, where they run ads for a nominal fee.

A source you might not have thought of is local or statewide newsletters. If you know of a guild or quilting organization that has a newsletter, you might approach the editor to see if you can run an ad. Sometimes editors will not only let you run an ad, but they may do a short story on you and your business.

When thinking about your ad, you will have to decide what information you want to include and, for the most part, design the ad yourself. Newspapers and magazines do have people who can design your ad for you, but it will cost you.

Business Papers

Another option to get the word out about your business is writing your own newsletter or putting together some brochures and/or fliers. If you have a website with an associated mailing list, you may already be writing a newsletter once a month and sending it out electronically. If you do, I wouldn't worry about doing a hard-copy one unless you want to print off the virtual one and leave it in fabric or quilting stores.

You can also create brochures and fliers to leave around town or at local events you attend. You can make a three-fold brochure, or if you teach classes, you can fold an 8½ x 11 sheet of paper in half and put your business information and an article, pattern, or recipe on the front and back and include a calendar with your class schedule in the middle.

Another option is using just one third of an 8½ x 11 page (so that you have three full ads on one printed sheet). This may be all the space you need to get the word out about your business. On one side you could put your contact information and what your business sells. On the other, you could list your classes or events you will be attending. The upside of doing this type of brochure or flier is you may print one hundred copies, but when they are cut, you'll wind up with three hundred. Some business owners use ads of this size as bookmarks, so you might want to print your copies on card stock.

You can design and make the master copy yourself. Then take the master down to a copy store and have as many copies as you want made. Color costs more than black and white and can get quite pricey, so if you are thinking about adding color to your copy, check the prices first. An alternative to color print is colored paper. This will only cost you a fraction of what the colored ink would cost.

Thinking out of the Box

While ads, newsletters, and brochures may be familiar forms of advertising to you, below are some different forms that you may not have thought about. Some can be very expensive, while others may cost you a nominal fee for a one-time effort. Check around for pricing and always be on the lookout for sales and unique forms of advertising that will help your business grow.

Bulletin Boards

Look around in your area and see which community locations have bulletin boards where individuals can put up cards or signs advertising their business. Libraries, laundromats, grocery stores, and even some gas stations have bulletin boards where you can display information. Where I live, the local pharmacy and liquor stores have huge bulletin boards where people tack business cards, garage sale signs, and more.

You will of course, want to be respectful of your host and not fill up the entire board with your information, but it is there for the community, so you might as well take advantage of it. Check back often. Sometimes people will take your cards or signs because they don't have anything with them to write down the information. Other times, the information just gets removed on a weekly, monthly, or quarterly basis.

Vehicle Signs

This may require a little bit of an investment, but once you get your signs made, you don't have to worry about further cost. Consider getting a magnetic vehicle sign that you can put on your car and easily remove later if need be, or purchase plastic sheets with your business information that you can fit in your vehicle windows.

How big you make your vehicle sign will depend on how much money you have to spend. You want at least enough room to include your business logo, name, phone number, and website. Vistaprint has some pretty good prices.

Yard Signs

Some people utilize yard signs to advertise their business. These don't have to be huge; the size of a realtor's sign is ideal. Once again, prices will vary according to size, type, colors involved, and construction. If you can find a company to make you a metal one, a one-time investment is probably all it will take. However, if you go with card-stock signs, you'll probably have to reinvest after the first rain.

Make sure to check with your homeowners association before you invest in yard signs. They may not allow any type of business signs in the yard no matter the size or how tasteful.

Premiums

If you attend festivals, art shows, or other events, you might want to think about purchasing some premiums to take and give away. Premiums are items like pens, rulers, cups, or magnets that have your business name, website, and phone number printed on them. Even if you can't attend a certain event, you can send premiums to be dropped in event packets and bags. You can find hundreds of premium offerings by doing an Internet search for "promotional business premiums." Items will range in price from two cents apiece and up. Know in advance, though, that the two-cent items may come with a quantity stipulation. For instance, you may have to buy one thousand pieces to get the two-cent price.

Don't get overwhelmed with all the options. Choose one or two and see how it works out. You might try a six-inch plastic ruler or a small sewing kit to represent your business. Let your budget be your guide. A few places that offer competitive prices are premsplus.com and nationalpen.com. When you do decide what you want to do, check and compare prices on these two websites. In the end, you may decide you can't afford to do any premiums, and that's okay.

Tracking What Works and What Doesn't

To help you keep an eye on where your marketing dollars are going, fill out the following marketing report on a regular basis. You don't have to do everything suggested in this chapter in one month, but perhaps try out one thing one month, see how it works, and then maybe something new the next month. If you have set a marketing budget, you'll be steps ahead of your competition.

After filling out the month and your budget amount, you'll want to write down what kind of marketing you did in the first column. Did you go to a chamber of commerce function? Did you attend a fair or festival? In the next column, describe what you did there. Did you meet people? Pass out business cards? Give away premiums? In the next two columns, record how much it cost you and what the results were. Did you join the organization you attended? How much were the dues? If you created premiums, how many did you pass out? Did you get a new client? Make some sales? Get some leads? Review your efforts month to month to see which ones are paying off.

Marketing Report

Month of _____ 20_____

Budget:_____

Type of Marketing	Description	Cost	Results

Comments: _____

_____

_____

09 Expanding Your Business

After you've been in business for a while, you may start questioning whether you should stay where you are, get a brick-and-mortar store, or simply call it quits. If you are doing well, making money at home, doing what you like to do with no pressure, why mess with a good thing? If you have been selling items from your home or teaching classes and more and more of your clients want to come by, or if the place where you've been holding classes starts charging you more than what you've been paying, you might want to look into moving your business out of your home and into a more traditional business setting. However, if you have grown tired of what you are doing, you've begun another phase of your life, or your business has become a burden instead of something you enjoy, you might want to call it quits.

In this chapter, we're going to explore the pros and cons of expanding your business. No matter when you decide to make a move or stay put, the decision is yours and yours alone. When you started your home business, you were probably focused on making money. While you no doubt have made money, if you are looking to make more, you need to think about expanding. It is not a decision that should be made lightly or quickly. Expanding a business will cost you money, time, and energy.

If you are unsure about expansion, don't do it. When it is the right time, you'll know it. Perhaps it never will be. Maybe you like the pace you've set, and you're fine with other changes you see going on around you. Time is on your side. Maybe a few years down the road, you'll see the business differently and want to go in a different direction.

Are You Ready To Expand?

You may have immediately answered yes to this question, but you need to stop and think about how this will affect not only your life, but your business finances, your health, and your family relationships. You may be thinking that when you expand, you can make more money. This is true, but you'll need to weigh this benefit with what it costs you in other areas of your life.

Before you read any further, take the self-test below. Put a mark beside each statement you can answer affirmatively.

If you put a check beside all ten questions, then you are ready to move forward. If you marked any fewer, you need to step back, take a look at those areas, and ask yourself why you couldn't mark them. This is a good time to check personal growth. Can you be honest with yourself and face the truth, or would you rather shove certain shortcomings under a rug? If you do the latter, you could face trouble down the road.

Before you move any further, let's look at a few areas from the checklist. They are crucial to the success or failure of your business.

Self-Test: Expanding Your Business

_____1)   I am healthy and ready for a new challenge.

_____2)   I have money set aside for the expansion and to purchase more product.

_____3)   I have enough contracted projects and already-made products to open a store and hire a few employees.

_____4)   I am excited and want to take advantage of opportunities presented to me.

_____5)   I have new endeavors I want to incorporate into the business expansion.

_____6)   I can stay focused on my business without becoming distracted.

_____7)   I have a clear vision of where I want my business to go (i.e., I have a business plan).

_____8)   I have written down what I need to do and what needs to happen to get my business to the next level.

_____9)   My current business is healthy, solid, and ready to expand.

_____10) I have the support of my family, friends, and colleagues.

Do You Have the Money to Expand?

If you are thinking about expanding, be it to another building on your property or another location entirely, you will need money to do it. Besides rent to pay, there will be utilities like water, electric, and phone or cable depending on your location. You will have to find shelving, and if you have been selling items strictly online, you will need to house items in your shop for people to pick up, buy, and carry out. With the expansion, you will probably need at least one or two full-time employees. All these costs will add up. You should at least have enough money set aside to carry you six months—or longer if you can swing it.

You might be thinking about getting a loan to help you with the move. That's fine, but talk to your accountant and your banker. See what it will cost you in the long run. It might not be worth it.

Are You in Good Health?

Remember all the work you did when you first started your home business. Now multiply that by ten. You will be working long hours again, maybe getting little sleep, there could be a commute, and things simply won't be as convenient as they were when you were home. Will you have enough energy to do everything you need to do to expand your business?

If you have already been feeling tired or if you are experiencing health problems, maybe you are just feeling your age, but now is not the time to add more stress to your life. You need to be healthy and full of energy to get everything done. Starting your business took a lot of work in the beginning. So will this new venture.

Do You Have the Support of Family and Friends?

How does your significant other feel about your business getting larger? If you have children, how do they feel about the change? Have friends voiced concerns or are they cheering you on? If your significant other or children have mentioned they would like to spend more time with you and you are getting ready to give them less, they will not be happy. An unhappy family makes for a very unhappy life. When you get started on expanding your business, you will need 100 percent support from every family member and friend you can find.

Reasons for Growing Your Business

Maybe your business has taken off, you've outgrown your space, and you really don't have a choice. You have to get out of your current location, hire more help, and get more products. If this is the case, great. But maybe you've thought if you get bigger, you'll make more money. That's a possibility, but you have to consider the alternative as well. If you have managed your business well, you will likely continue to make money, but if you aren't successful now, think about what you are doing and why it hasn't worked.

As you grow, you will have more and more responsibility, not less. Your business will always need your oversight and input. Don't think as you hire employees that you can leave your business in their hands. That's the quickest way to destroy it.

Maybe the direction of your business has changed. Maybe you have students who have taken your classes for years and now you'd like to bring in guest speakers, not only for them, but because you want to learn new things. Maybe you have decided you want to sell more quilt kits and the patterns you design rather than completed quilts. Or maybe you've decided you would rather deal with people face to face on a daily basis than on the phone or Internet.

If you think expanding your business can be fun, remember the hard work and challenges you will be facing. Think about how excited you were when you started your business at the very beginning. You should be just as excited now.

You will also need to stay focused. There will be a lot of changes with an expanding business, more things you have to do and keep track of. If you have recently faced or are currently facing a family or personal crisis like a death, divorce, or other situation, you might want to rethink the timing of your expansion. Give it a few months. Let your head clear so you can think clearly about your business and everything you need to do.

Whatever your reasons for expanding, make sure you write them down and think long and hard before you rent a space or order three hundred pairs of scissors.

How Are You Looking to Expand?

This is just as important to consider as the reasons you are expanding. If you are thinking about adding more products to your home business, that's one thing. If you are talking about moving out of the home to another location entirely, that's something else. The amount of change you make will determine whether you need to make minor or major changes.

For example, if you have decided to move to an outbuilding on your property, there will certainly be work, but it won't be as difficult as moving the business across town. The same is true about your workload. Depending on what you want to do will determine the amount of work involved.

Increasing Your Numbers

Maybe your expansion is not so much a move but a matter of numbers. Let's say you sell quilt kits and average ten quilt kit sales a month. You want to double that number in two months and then double that in another two months, so that by the end of the year, you are selling at least fifty quilt kits a month on a regular basis.

This is doable, but you need to have a plan. If you intend to sell that many kits, you have to have that many kits made up to sell. That means you will have to buy materials and packaging supplies to make up the kits and possibly hire some help to cut and package. Whatever you do, you need to think ahead and plan not only your time, but your money as well.

Beyond Design

When Rhonda Ponder and her daughter, Melissa Ott-Herman, started Quilteroos in Ruston, Louisiana, they had already been quilting for many years. Rhonda had run a home-based quilting business since 1999. In early 2012, she and Melissa took the leap to move out of her home and into town. "The quilt shop owner had been here since the 1970s, and she was retiring," Melissa says. "It was a natural fit and the right time for us to move into a quilt shop in town. We opened in April 2012."

Changing Locations

If you have decided you want to move out of your home and into another building, there are many things to think about. How much is it going to cost? So far, you may have been paying for phone and Internet service and maybe a few other utilities, but when you move, you will also have rent or a mortgage payment if you are buying a building. On top of that you will have the utilities and insurance. You will need to protect your investment in case of fire and robbery. If any remodeling needs to be done, you will need to factor that in as well.

Once you get the building secure, as mentioned before, you will need shelving and product to sell. You need to give people a reason to come into your establishment, and when they do, you want them to spend money to help you meet your expenses.

Another consideration when moving into town is how accessible your shop will be and whether or not there is ample parking. If people can't find you or if your location is difficult to reach, they may not come. If parking is a hassle, they may decide it's not worth the effort and leave before they've even come in your store to see what you have to offer.

If you need to expand but don't want to move in to town, why not expand on your own property if you have enough room? That's what several quilting business owners have done. You may need to get a zoning permit and permission from your homeowner's association, but it can be done and quite successfully.

Joan Knight of Quilts and Things decided she liked keeping her business close to home, so she and her husband built a 60 x 40 metal barn at the back of their property where she now works, holds classes, and more. "It has air-conditioning, microwave, small icebox, bathroom, design wall—all the comforts," Joan says. "I love it."

Whichever way you decide to go, think ahead and plan for unexpected expenses and demands on your time.

Bringing More Help on Board

You might have so much work that you need to bring on some full-time and part-time employees. Maybe that is your goal for expanding. If so, consider the cost. What will the employees be doing? How much can you pay them? Can you keep them busy, especially your full-timers?

If you are thinking about hiring full-time employees, try one at the beginning. If that one works out and you have valuable part-time help, maybe choose another full-timer from that pool of workers. You already have your part-time help trained, and this will save you time and money in the long run.

Expanding Your Services

Maybe you've been making quilt tops for people and then sending them out to be longarm-quilted by someone else. After you've added up what it's been costing you, you've decided to start not only doing your own quilts, but finishing up quilts for others too. You've looked at the prices of longarm machines and decided how, when, and where you are going to get the word out about your venture. You are ready to go.

This is just one of the ways you can expand your services. If you've just made small items in the past, why not break into making bigger items and vice versa? Maybe you've been making quilts for people and the pattern has become quite popular. Why not put together some kits of that pattern and try selling those?

If you get creative and think about it, there are many different ways you can take the business, expand it and continue to make money. Moving away from your home and setting up shop somewhere else is one way to go, but not the only way.

Knowing When It's Time to Move On

There comes a time in everyone's business life when they get tired, burned out, and simply need to move on or call it quits. Everyone typically knows when that time comes. You can feel it in your heart and soul. Doing what you once loved has now become a burden. The excitement is gone. Each day becomes a test of endurance, and by the end of the day you're not sure if you can face the next.

Maybe it's not that you're tired or bored, but it's time for you to retire. You and your significant other have saved up enough money to buy a home in the mountains or by the ocean, and you plan on spending a lot of time there relaxing with the grandkids. You know that running your business will be difficult when you are away, so you've decided to cut back or even call it quits.

Beyond Design

"We are trying to phase out our business now," Pearl Harris of Pearl's Quilts says. "My husband and I are seventy-eight, and we're ready to retire."

Another reason to call the business quits is if you get in over your head financially and it begins making you sick. When you first started out, it wasn't your intention to close your business down for financial reasons, but it happens. It would be better to cut the strings of the balloon and let it fly away. That way you could get on with your life rather than drag everything out. If you hold on for too long, things could end up the same way, except with you stuck in the hospital.

Depending on where you are and what you are thinking, you do have some options. If you are truly ready to call it quits, you could put your business up for sale. You could find a buyer and add the money from the sale to your retirement fund. That way your customers wouldn't be left out in the cold and what you started could continue. You could also pass your business on to your children if they are interested in what you've been doing and want to continue the tradition. Another option, especially if you just need a break from the business, is to take on a partner or two. You could stay on as an executive member in an advisory position. You may eventually want to sell the business to your partners, but for now this might be an alternative.

Finally, when you are facing this decision, look back over the reason you started your business. You wanted to be your own boss, have fun, run your business the way you wanted to, and call your own shots. Because the business is yours, you can decide how you want to end it just like you decided how to start it. No matter what you decide to do, make sure your decision is the best for you, and when you go to bed at night you can close your eyes with no regrets, knowing you did it your way.

Appendix A: General Resources

In the appendices that follow, you will find information on the artists, business owners, and the resources mentioned in this book. Other educational resources, quilting organizations, and suppliers, are given too. You may never use any resource on this list, but if you happen to need one or two, then my work to build it will have been well worth it.

This by no means is a complete list. Additionally, every day new websites go up, new books are published, and another company decides to get in the business of building quilt machines. My hope is that you use these appendices as a starting point. As you grow your business, you will grow your list of contacts and resources too. Google is an excellent starting point. You will be amazed at the information you can find by simply looking on the Web. Don't forget your community resources as well. There are lots available to you.

I wish you all the best with your business and happy quilting no matter what you quilt.

Accounting Programs

ABC Inventory Software: almyta.com/abc_inventory_software.asp
EZ Small Business: allprosoftware.com/ez/
Inflow Inventory: inflowinventory.com
Intuit: intuit.com
NetSuite: netsuite.com
POS Maid: firstmerchantservices.com
Quickbooks: quickbooks.intuit.com
Quicken: quicken.intuit.com
Sage Accounting: na.sage.com

Artists and Business Owners Mentioned in This Book

Betsy's Quilts
Betty Hairfield
HC 83 Box 870
Antlers, OK 74523
(580) 298-5821
Betty and her small number of employees make and finish quilts for customers. Her customers drop off, mail, or ship their quilt tops for her to work on while other customers come by to tell her what they want her to make for them. Currently, she has no website. She's been too busy to put one up.

Creative Stitching & Design
Karen Niemi
creative.stitching.home.comcast.net
creative.stitching@comcast.net
(303) 470-9309
Karen designs, makes, and sells quilts of her own and finishes quilts for customers. Her quilts have been featured in magazines and exhibited at fairs, festivals, and the Colorado State Capitol. Check out her website to learn more about her work and to contact her.

Devoted to Quilting
Nita Beshear
devotedtoquilting.wordpress.com/
nita@nitabeshear.com
Nita is an author, speaker, and quilt maker. From her home in southeastern Oklahoma, she sews together not only pieces of fabric to make quilts, but sews together words to create stories about those who make quilts and those who receive them.

Heaven's Quilts
Rita Meyerhoff
heavensquilts.com
rita@heavensquilts.com
15725 W 63rd Ave.
Arvada, CO 80403
(720) 219-8169

Rita sees clients by appointment only. She designs and makes quilts and finishes them for her customers. She teaches at various locations and also does one-on-one classes by special appointment. Her work is exhibited at fairs and festivals regularly and at the Golden Quilt Museum in Golden, Colorado.

Pearl's Quilts
Pearl and Everett Harris
pearlsquilts.com
epharris@junct.com
32298 S 4505 Rd.
Afton, OK 74331
(918) 782-9350

Husband and wife Everett and Pearl Harris run their quilting business from their country home in far eastern Oklahoma. While Pearl is the designer of the pair, Everett holds the reins of the Singer quilting machine. They finish quilts for clients and make and sell their own designs.

Quilteroo's
Rhonda Ponder and Melissa Ott-Herman
quilteroo.com
quilteroo@yahoo.com
1309 Farmerville Hwy
Ruston, LA 71270
(318) 255-0992

Mother and daughter team Rhonda and Melissa run this business from a storefront location. The business used to be located in Rhonda's home, but when the opportunity arose to purchase a building, she and daughter Melissa jumped on the chance. They sell fabric, thread, and notions, and they are a Brother sewing and embroidery machine retailer. They continue to make quilts and teach others how to make them too.

Quilts and Things
Joan Knight
quiltsandthings.info
jnknight@bellsouth.net
2115 Forest Ridge Rd.
Prattville, AL 36067
(334) 358-7827
Being a Stitch-n-Frame Gammill sub-dealership would be enough to keep Joan busy year-round, but she does more. She makes quilts and finishes quilts for clients plus teaches classes at the national level. When she's not traveling around the country teaching, you can find Joan in her barn beta-testing a program for Creative Studio or working on her quilting videos.

Theresa May Quilts
Theresa May
theresemay.com
therese@theresemay.com
1556 Wawona Dr.
San Jose, CA 95125
(866) 292-3247
Therese, an artist and quilter, likes to combine her two passions to create stunning works of fabric art that sell for thousands of dollars. On any given day you might find her painting on fabric or adding beadwork to her designs. Her work has been exhibited at the Smithsonian Institute in Washington, DC, as well as at the Louvre in Paris, France. She also teaches classes and speaks at various conferences and festivals.

Education
American Quilt Study Group (AQSG)
americanquiltstudygroup.org
This organization's main office is located in Lincoln, Nebraska. Its goal is to preserve, maintain, and assimilate quilting history and heritage information and

keep it alive for generations to come. If you want to do some self-education, tapping into this group's resources can be a place to start. The AQSG has access to over five thousand volumes of research material located in the University of Nebraska library.

Baylor University
baylor.edu
Located in Waco, Texas, this is one of many colleges that offer quilting classes as part of a four-year degree. Baylor has a bachelor's of fine arts in textiles. While you won't be quilting all the time, you will learn the nuances of fabric and fibers.

Fashion Institute of Technology
fitnyc.edu
This institute is located in New York City and gives lots of hands-on experience to students interested in studying fabric design and styling. The school offers an associate of applied science degree and a bachelor of fine arts degree in textile/surface design. Students also get the opportunity to study abroad in Canada, England, and France.

Michigan State University
msu.edu
This four-year university is located in East Lansing, Michigan. The school offers a four-year bachelor's of fine arts in apparel and textile design. Students will study the history of textiles and take a hands-on approach to design.

Quilt History Resources
quilthistory.com
This organization has small study groups located in different states. These groups get together and share quilt histories, experiences, and restoration efforts.

The Studio Art Quilt Associates
saqa.com
This is a nonprofit organization whose goal is to promote quilt art through education, documentation, exhibitions, and more. The website features a long list of universities that offer fiber art degree programs. You will no doubt be able to find one close to you.

Quilting Machines

American Professional Quilting Systems: apqs.com

Gammill: gammill.net

Nolting: nolting.com/Index.php

Sewing Machines

Baby Lock: babylock.com

Bernina of America, Inc.: bernina.com/en-US

Brother International: brother-usa.com/homesewing

Elna: elnausa.com/en-us/

Husqvarna Viking: new.husqvarnaviking.com/en-US

Janome: content.janome.com/index.cfm/machines

Juki: jukihome.com/

Pfaff: pfaffusa.com/

Spencer Sewing Machine Company: spencersewing.com/sewing.php

Suppliers

Aurifil: aurifil.com

Black & Decker: blackanddecker.com

Bohin France: bohin.fr/en

Clover: clover-usa.com

Coats & Clark: coatsandclark.com

Collins: dritz.com/brands/collins/index.php

Creative Grids USA: creativegridsusa.com

Dritz Prym Consumer USA Inc.: dritz.com

Fiskars: www3.fiskars.com

Fons & Porter's: fonsandporter.com/index.html

Ginghern Scissors and Shears: gingher.com

Gutermann: guetermann.com/shop/en/view/content

Havel's Sewing: havelssewing.com

Olfa: olfa.com/splash.aspx

Oliso: oliso.com/

Omnigrid: dritz.com/brands/omnigrid

OttLite: ott-lite.com

Panasonic North America: panasonic.com/us/home

Pinmoor: pinmoor.com

Robison-Anton: robison-anton.com

Rowenta: rowentausa.com/pages/default.aspx

Uline: uline.com

X-ACTO: xacto.com/Home.aspx

Website Templates

Free Web Templates: freetemplates.com

Open Source Templates: opensourcetemplates.org

WIX: wix.com

Websites: Domain Name Registration, Hosting, and More

Blog: blog.com

Blogger: blogger.com

Etsy: etsy.com

Go Daddy: godaddy.com

Network Solutions: networksolutions.com

Register: register.com

Simple Site: simplesite.com

Top 10 Online Store Builders: top10onlinestorebuilders.com

Webs: webs.com

Wordpress: wordpress.com

Appendix B:
Marketing Resources

Advertising Resources
Business Cards and Flyers
Next Day Flyers: nextdayflyers.com

Overnight Prints: overnightprints.com

Staples: staples.com

Vista Print: vistaprint.com

Business Directories
National
AtList: atlist.org

Biz Journal: businessdirectory.bizjournals.com/claim/add

Dex: dexknows.com

Google: google.com

Manta: manta.com

Merchant Circle: merchantcircle.com/signup

Universal Business Listing: ubl.org

Yellow Pages: yellowpages.com

Yelp: yelp.com

Local
City Search: citysearch.com

Insider Pages: insiderpages.com

Local: local.com

Yahoo Local: local.yahoo.com

The Web Map: thewebmap.com

Show Me Local: showmelocal.com/businessregistration.aspx

Miscellaneous

Block Central: blockcentral.com

Creative Crafts Groups: creativecraftsgroup.com

Daytimers: daytimers.com

Digital Camera Information: digitalcamerainfo.com

Franklin Planner: franklinplanner.com

Independent Insurance Agents and Brokers of America: iiaba.net

Neat Scanning Machines: neat.com

Quilts for Kids: quiltsforkids.org

Quilts for Vets: kellytrudell.net/vetsupport/quiltsforvets.html

Quilts of Honor: quiltsofhonor.org

Quilts of Valor: qovf.org

Rocky Mountain Quilt Museum: rmqm.org

Quilt Web: quiltweb.com

Quiltbug: quiltbug.com

The Quilting Board: The Quilter's Message Board: quiltingboard.com

Quilts Inc.: quilts.com

Studio Arts Quilts Association: saqa.com

Signs, Premiums, and More

Direct Mail: directmail.com

National Pen Co.: nationalpen.com

Postcard Mania: postcardmania.com

Premiums Plus Incorporated: premiumsplus.com

Sign Depot: yardsignwholesale.com

Vistaprint: vistaprint.com

Social Networks

Facebook: facebook.com

Instagram: instagram.com

LinkedIn: linkedin.com

Pinterest: pinterest.com

Tumblr: tumblr.com

Twitter: twitter.com

YouTube: youtube.com

Appendix C:
Organizations and Guilds

American Quilter's Society
PO Box 3290
Paducah, KY 42002-3290
(270) 898-7903
americanquilter.com
This society is a quilt book and magazine publisher, and it is also a membership organization. In the group's own words, it is "a forum for quilters of all skill levels." Not only does the society offer books and magazines, but it also holds quilt contests, quilt shows, and quilting workshops throughout the year. For a twenty-five-dollar membership fee, you subscribe to this group's magazine for a year.

Better Business Bureau
bbb.org
This organization is the watchdog of business and business scams. If you have a problem or complaint about a business, you can report it to the Better Business Bureau. You can also contact the BBB about getting your business accredited. They won't help you sell anything related to your business, but they will help you gain consumers' trust.

International Quilt Association
7660 Woodway Dr., Suite 550
Houston, TX 77063
(713) 781-6882
quilts.org
Established in 1979, this nonprofit organization is dedicated to preserving quilting as an art form. No guilds are associated with this group; members

join individually. The group holds a judged show every year whose top prize is ten thousand dollars. Visit the association's website to learn more about what it does and how it can help your business.

National Association of Women Business Owners
601 Pennsylvania Avenue NW
South Building, Suite 900
Washington, DC 20004
(800) 556-2926
nawbo.org
Founded in 1975, this group grew from twelve members to thousands. Its goal is to help women business owners by strengthening their knowledge of government issues that may affect them as female business owners and promote economic development within the women's business sphere. The association looks for a diverse membership and values all members who empower women entrepreneurs.

National Quilt Guilds
quilt.net
If you are looking for a list of quilt shows or groups in your area, check out this site first. It has a long list of sites that may help you find what you are looking for.

National Quilting Association
nqaquilts.org
This national organization was founded in 1970 by seven women who wanted to keep the art of quilting alive. Over the years, the association has launched many programs that help quilters new and old learn about the history of quilts, the art of quilting, and the maintenance and preservation of quilts already made. This organization offers grants to qualifying individuals and holds quilt shows and other events throughout the year that help its members. Memberships start at twenty-five dollars.

Quilt Guilds Worldwide
quiltguilds.com
Looking for a quilt guild or group to join? Check out this site. If you can't find a guild here, there might not be one. This site covers groups and guilds in the United States, Canada, Japan, Australia, New Zealand, France, Africa, the United Kingdom, and other countries.

US Small Business Administration (SBA)

409 Third St. SW

Washington, DC 20416

sba.gov

Founded in 1953, this independent government agency has been helping businesses through business financing, business education, technical training, dispensing business information, and business advocacy. It has offices throughout the country, so business owners everywhere can get help when starting a business or expanding an existing one. The agency offers classes throughout the year at different locations on different business practices. The Service Corps of Retired Executives (SCORE) is a resource partner of the SBA. You can link to SCORE's website off of the SBA's site or visit it directly at score.org.

Appendix D:
Festivals and Shows

This is only a small list of festivals and shows located around the country. Start building your own list by looking at some of the directories listed below. Contact the groups' organizers to find out how to enter your quilt in the judged portion of the show and how to get your quilts exhibited at festivals.

Directories
American Quilters Society Quilt Shows: asqsshows.com
Quilt Festivals: quiltfest.com
Quilting Pathways: quiltingpathways.com

Festivals and Shows
Firehouse Quilts of Colorado Shows: firehousequilts.org
International Quilt Festival: quilts.com
Lowell Quilt Festival: lowellquiltfestival.org
Oklahoma Winter Quilt Show: centralokquilters.org
Sisters Outdoor Quilt Show: sistersoutdoorquiltshow.org
Walla Walla Valley Quilt Festival: wallawallaquiltfestival.org

Appendix E:
Books You Might Find Helpful

Cox, Meg. *The Quilter's Catalog.* New York, NY: Workman Publishing Company, 2008. This 597-page book will keep you flipping pages for hours. It covers everything from snippets of quilting information to festivals to explaining what a log cabin quilt consists of. There is also a section on different teachers and quilters who have been in the business a long time.

Darling, Sharon. *Quilter's Review Guide to Finding a Sewing Machine You'll Love.* Andover, NH: Trillium Publishing, 2003. This small book is packed full of information. Maybe the best part is the survey you get to fill out to see what kind of machine you really want. It will definitely get you thinking.

Marshall, Kathy, and Judy Turner. *How to Start Your Own Machine Quilting Business.* quiltingbusiness.com/machinequiltbiz.htm: Gruntled Enterprises, 2004. Even though this spiral-bound book is only available on the Internet, you might want to check it out. It discusses the ins and outs of starting a longarm quilting business.

Other Books to Consider

Bell, Mark William. *Build a Website for Free.* Indianapolis, Indiana: QUE, 2009.

Brown, Bruce C. *How to Build Your Own Website with Little or No Money: The Complete Guide for Business and Personal Use.* Ocala, Florida: Atlanta Publishing Group, 2010.

Falcone, Paul. *The Hiring & Firing Question and Answer Book.* New York: AMA-COM, 2001.

Lynch, Liz. *102 Secrets to Smarter Networking*. New York: Consult Ad Hoc, 2003.

———. *Smart Networking: Attract a Following in Person and Online*. New York: McGraw-Hill, 2008.

Rassas, Lori B. *Employment Law: A Guide to Hiring, Managing, and Firing for Employers and Employees*. New York: Aspen Publishers, 2010.

Sansevieri, Penny C. *Red Hot Internet Publicity*. New York: Cosimo Books, 2009.

Schenck, Barbara Findlay. *Small Business Marketing for Dummies*. Hoboken, New Jersey: John Wiley and Sons, Inc., 1020.

Sernovitz, Andy. *Word of Mouth Marketing: How Smart Companies Get People Talking*. New York: Kaplan Press, 2009.

Index

About the Author

Deborah Bouziden has been writing and publishing books and articles since 1983. During that time she has lost track of how many articles she's published, but her friends keep track of her books and tell her she's had sixteen published so far, six for Globe Pequot Press. She has written fiction and nonfiction, specializing in nonfiction how-tos.

She travels across the country and speaks about writing in general and, when she gets the time, holds writing seminars in her local communities of Edmond, Oklahoma, and Estes Park, Colorado.

Currently, she is working on a proposal on how to write how-tos while continuing to promote her books. To learn more about Bouziden, visit her website at deborahbouziden.com.